Death

Thierry Malleret

This is a work of fiction.
Any resemblance to actual or past events
and individuals is purely coincidental.

Edition 1.0

Thierry Malleret
Chemin de la Croix des Pècles
74400 Chamonix Mont-Blanc
France

ISBN : 978-2-9592936-0-3

From The Same Author

The Great Narrative (with Klaus Schwab)
Forum Publishing, 2022 – essay

The Great Reset (with Klaus Schwab)
Forum Publishing, 2020 – essay

Dix bonnes raisons d'aller marcher
Paulsen, 2017 – essay

Les riches sont-ils méchants ?
Slatkine, 2013 – novel

Six Global Mega Trends and How to Make Them Work For You
Versilio, 2013 – essay

Disequilibrium – A World Out of Kilter
Bookbaby, 2012 – essay

Global Risk – Business Success in Turbulent Times (with Sean Cleary)
Palgrave Macmillan, 2007 – essay

Crimes sans châtiments
Maxima, 2002 – novel

La roulette russe
Le Rocher, 1998, novel

Alerte aux fous de Dieu
Flammarion, 1997 – novel

Le montage caucasien
Le Rocher, 1996 – novel

Conversion of the Defense Industry in the Former Soviet Union
Institute for East-West security Studies, 1991 – essay

L'armée rouge Face à la perestroïka
Complexe, 1991 – essay

Table of Contents

FOREWORD

This short geopolitical thriller is a work of fiction (any resemblance to actual or past events and individuals is purely coincidental), and the overture of a series of "collaborative novels" with sequels to be published.

Authors, experts, and journalists from varied backgrounds are invited to contribute to the sequels, which, like "Deaths at Davos", will shed light, through fiction and its power of imagination, on some very real issues of global relevance.

If you are tempted to contribute, all ideas and suggestions are welcome.
Please get in touch at deathsatdavos@gmail.com.

Day 1

Saturday 13 January 2024
From Zurich To Davos

Nobody ever said it would be easy.

This was the thought uppermost in Olena's mind as she boarded the train. The next few days would be a trial by fire. Nothing light-hearted or frivolous was on the menu. Only problems, frustration, and too many rounds of tough, hopeless negotiations. There'd be a few surprises, for sure, and plenty of gossip. Small talk rumours and tittle-tattle. All quintessential features of the Circle's yearly gathering in Davos. As an ex-Circle-employee she knew the circus inside out. But this year was different: she was returning as an official participant armed with a much-coveted white badge and its all-important passepartout little chip – the hologrammed badge of honour that provided full access to everything that mattered. The exclusive domain of just a very happy few. And yet... she wasn't looking forward to it. How could she be? Her country was in a bloody mess. The world was in a mess. She was on her way to negotiate a series of impossible agreements at the worst possible moment. Just when hope had started to fade.

She took a seat in the middle of the carriage, in first class - a bit of an indulgence by her own modest standards but one that could pass for virtue-signalling among other white badge holders who typically travelled to the Circle's annual jamboree by private plane, helicopter or chauffeured Mercedes-Benz. Besides, she needed some peace and quiet. Some calm before the storm. She placed on the table the two (it was a long journey) cups of coffee she'd just bought at Starbucks on the platform in Zurich and pulled out her copy of Vladimir Sorokin's "Day of the Oprichnik", which she wanted to finish before Landquart, the station where she would change for the local train to Davos-Platz. But the comfortable carriage was warm and welcoming. Her eyelids were heavy. Which would win - sleep or Sorokin? Sleep, probably. Already she was drifting off, lost in thoughts of the days ahead.

She was in two minds. What could she possibly achieve? The pluses: forging great connections within the global elite holed-up in an isolated and splendid corner of the Swiss Alps for a week. The good and the great. Thousands of doers, thinkers, shapers, and leaders to toy with. Not easy, as networking meant networking "up". Nobody was interested in connecting "down". Up, up, up! Always up – an impossible, exhausting, transactional game, but she'd do her best and was damn good at it. The minuses: she was under no illusion. No one was there to improve the state of the world, let alone the state of her own country. A journalist had dubbed Davos "a family reunion for the people who broke the modern world." There was some truth in that. The Circle was a handsomely upholstered comfort zone for people who had already changed the world, not necessarily for the better, and now wanted to cover their tracks. How come? This was the way it was designed and managed, and above all there was a golden operating rule: never upset anybody who paid to come. A rule even more stringent vis-à-vis the financial partners who coughed up a fortune to be there. You could question somebody's facts, but you could never question their honesty, their motivation or their importance. Put another way, always caress their egos. As a former employee, Olena understood what that meant: chitchat as much as you want about the big issues of the day – the climate emergency, social justice, inequalities, transparency, tech governance, peace or whatever – but never, ever, disrupt the status quo. And never, ever, make anybody feel uncomfortable... That said, an incident could always occur. Like in 2019 when a young Dutch academic went off-piste by suggesting that people in Davos could not only save the world, and along with it capitalism's reputation, by paying more taxes. He'd caused a bit of a stir, like an unruly child burping at the grown-up dinner table. Never reinvited.

The truth be known, serious tax reform proposals like a Global Assets Register or the creation of a UN tax convention had never found backing at the Circle and never would. Just too many vested interests. Olena pondered whether the same fate awaited this year's proposal for a new "taskforce on international taxation to scale up development, climate and nature action". The name could be snappier, but the idea, first floated at COP28, was a great one. Its logic seemed impeccable: since the $7 trillion annual fossil-fuel subsidies helped to fund the $4 trillion profit the oil and gas industry made in 2023, why not create a carbon tax on certain economic activities to raise climate and nature finance? Common sense, no? Taxing trade in fossil fuels or private jet travel, for example, would not harm the economy and would only come at the expense of those who could best afford it. Several countries had put this forward, and her own project could benefit from it. But she had her doubts. Too bold. Too contentious. Too taboo. The lobbyists who came in droves to Davos, hidden amongst the white badges, would tear it down. 'Lovely idea', they'd say, 'but sadly impossible to implement'. In effect, the Circle was a place where most people came to talk about things instead of doing them.

*****

The train left the underground platform. In the darkness of the tunnel, Olena gazed at her reflection in the window. Still alluring, but she'd aged. The unimaginable stress of the past two years had taken its toll on her youthful Slavic beauty and left dark circles under her bright green eyes. Yet, looking back at her from the window was comfortingly ample evidence that she remained powerfully attractive. As the train emerged into the daylight and left the last of the calm and elegant city behind, she looked out across the Zurichsee to the lush greenery of the foothills and the majestic silhouette of the Glarus Alps beyond. A magical moment, so tranquil. Undisturbed.

Until an obsequious voice broke the spell.

'Ms. Kostarenko?' said the voice coming from a bespectacled man with a sad face.

Olena glanced up with a look of surprise and thinly veiled irritation.

'Yes?'

'I am Alain Girard. We met on two or three occasions in London and Kiev.'

Now she remembered. A French hack who'd taken an ambiguous, if not hostile, stance vis-à-vis Ukraine since the beginning of Russia's war.

'Can I ask you a few questions?' he said. Without waiting for an answer, he sat down in front of her while placing his own Starbucks latte on her table.

'I am sorry, but I have a lot of reading to do just now, if you don't mind.'

The journalist wasn't going to give up.

'Just one question then. As a Ukrainian, where do you see President Zelenskyy in a year from now?'

'Leading his country and leading it well, Monsieur Girard. Forgive me but I have work to do.'

He glared at her, a look oscillating between reprobation and frustration. He too had a job to do, and his job was to talk to her, which made it hers to talk to him.

'Too bad', he said standing up and reclaiming his coffee. 'Well, another time. We have four days to discuss this project of yours', he said in a conspiratorial whisper.

'I think you've taken my coffee', observed Olena.

'Oh yes! Maybe.' He swapped it, without an apology.

Olena distractedly opened her book and looked around her. The carriage was packed with Circle-type people. Many looking as if they were about to embark on a polar expedition, judging from their apparel and the enormous suitcases cluttering the corridor. Several were talking too loudly, rather too pleased with the sound of their own voice. These were people accustomed to an audience. From the corner of her eye, she registered the sliding door opening at the end of the carriage. An innately confident and elegantly dressed man walked up the aisle, taking his time, his arms stretched out in front of him, finishing up a video call on his mobile phone. She recognised Karl Manhof, the young German multibillionaire with whom she'd be spending a good deal of time over the next few days. Manhof had inherited the family fortune amassed in coal mining, tripled it in tech before becoming infatuated with green investing. In 2021, he created a fund called "Go Green" in which he put a few hundred million of his own money, adding capital from friends and clients along the way. He was now managing a 5-billion-euro fund, branded and re-branded depending on the prevailing vibe as sustainable investing, impact investing, responsible investing, ESG, sustainable circularity; and more. At this very moment, it was "building COPitalism." He just followed the fashion. Go Green's motto: "Greening. Faster. Together." He normally flew his Falcon 900 and a fleet of helicopters, so Olena was mildly surprised to see him on her train. No doubt a publicity stunt. His staff already posting videos from his mobile phone on TikTok, YouTube, and LinkedIn as proof of his ongoing love affair with public transport. What admirable simplicity!

'Olenka, what a delightful surprise! You and me both walking the green talk on a Swiss train! Leading by example!' he declaimed emphatically.

What was he doing calling her by her affectionate diminutive? she thought. They'd met often, but only ever in a professional context. He was already annoying her in all the ways he always had. Pedantic, over-confident, self-centred.

'Good for you and well done us!' responded Olena with only thinly disguised sarcasm.

He sat in the same place Alain Girard had occupied a few minutes before, crossing his arms on the tray and bending towards Olena.

'So… Let's compare notes. What's on our 'to do' list for this week?'

'Big things! In three or four days from now, I will have negotiated some major infrastructure projects, and you'll invest in every one of them, earning a good return for yourself and doing good for Ukraine.'

'Exactly so! As I committed a month ago in Dubai during COP, my fund will not only finance your projects to the tune of 10% of all public donor contributions, but I will also bring many other private investors along for the ride.

I'm going to put your country back on its feet and do so in a sustainable manner. Go Green!' he almost shouted, a smug look on his face.

Olena wasn't sure. Did he mean it? From the outset, she'd found it odd that he wanted to get involved in the Reconstruct Ukraine fund. Like all tech investors who'd made loads of money, he always drank from a glass half-full and had a solution for everything, a claim not matched by his ability to convince others. Rumour had it that Go Green was floundering, with a few big investors having already taken their money out. And she'd been less than impressed in Dubai. In the few meetings they'd had with prospective investors he seemed to have a hard job even convincing himself of the pertinence of the project. He couldn't shift the air of a not-so-clever daddy's boy. Not great. This said, his impressive political connections across Europe and the US could surely prove useful to her project. Perhaps he was mulling a move into politics, hence his willingness to lead a coalition of investors and entrepreneurs to reconstruct Ukraine. Karl in a hard-hat reconstructing Ukraine would play better than Karl in a Hugo Boss suit shorting the euro? Or did he have some other ulterior motive?

Something wasn't quite right, although she couldn't put her finger on exactly what. But she also knew she couldn't do without him.

'Thank you, Karl,' she said.

The train came out of a tunnel, skirting the Wallensee lake. The view was breath-taking. A range of chiselled cliffs plunging into the inky dark water, while their tops flamed in the sunset's incandescence. For just a moment the two were silenced by the beauty of this natural spectacle. Then Karl turned his gaze to Olena.

'For sure we haven't chosen the easiest moment to invest.'

'Is there ever a good moment to invest when a country is at war?' she countered.

'You're not wrong! But Ukraine is in a particularly difficult situation just now. Today's timing may not be the best, but we can and will do it!'

'Yes, it's now we need your support, Karl. There is a window here and it may not stay open for ever. Above all we need the support of the US and Europe. Without them, there isn't much hope. In the end, it all depends on Trump.'

'What do you mean? What's Trump got to do with it?'

She looked back at the mountains. Then at him.

'From day one, Putin had banked on the US and Europe's lack of resolve, and on them tiring of the whole Ukrainian situation. He'd thought all along that time was on his side because the dissolute West would orchestrate its own demise. It seems he is now being proven right. We are at the point where both the US and Europe will fail to deliver enough assistance and enough weapons, the US because of political disputes in Congress, and the EU because of Orban, populists and 'fatigue'. But Congress or Hungary or populism, for us it's the same story, that of Trump's ideas gaining ground. Do you understand Karl? For

Ukraine, the possibility that this madman gets elected in November is terrifying because if he returns to power, we'll be in deep, terminal shit. Putin has been waiting for his victory for years and working hard to make it happen. He'll be delighted and vindicated that his friend Donald is back at the helm. This is when he'll gain the upper hand, for real, I mean. For us it will be a disaster, and for you, well… You can forget about your cosy European democracy and lifestyle.'

She stared at him. Intently.

'Now is the time to invest Karl. A year from now, it might be too late. Trump might be there.'

'Hmm', mumbled Karl, unsure of what to say and what to think. As far as he could tell, his American friends were telling him that the Donald had his issues but had been quite good for them as President.

He fidgeted in his seat, moving his hands across the table towards those of the young Ukrainian. Her reaction was to do the opposite.

'You said you needed my support Olenka. You have it, fully and unconditionally, but I also need yours…'

'What do you mean?'

'You remember our conversation in Dubai about my idea for an offsetting certification project. Well… I wanted to repeat that it would be a nice addition to your …'

She cut him off, and steely-eyed, retorted:

'I do Karl. I do remember our conversation. My position hasn't changed. You know that Ukraine doesn't have a carbon trading market yet. Until it has a clean and functioning one, I do not want to have one company in charge of certifying offsets, even if it's one of your companies. Certifying offsets in the current circumstances would be the royal road to corruption. And besides, I don't want to be accused of climate- or nature-washing. Most offsets are bullshit. Everybody knows that.'

'That's a bit harsh!'

'It isn't and you know it. We can set all the net zero targets we want, but if we can't track them, I'm not interested. And if we include in our calculations the use of offsets that are not measurable, forget it! Until we have a carbon trading market, there'll be no regulation, no accountability. It will be a trap, Karl. I don't want to fall into it.'

He threw her an imploring look.

'But your deputy was rather in favour of my idea at COP.'

'Maybe, but it's not my deputy who makes the final decision. It's me.'

*****

At that very moment, a kerfuffle broke out at the far end of the carriage. A group of passengers was gesticulating furiously, desperate to get everyone, anyone's attention. Olena and Karl stood up, hurriedly stepping over a suitcase to draw nearer. They were met by a vision of horror.

The French journalist was doubled up in agony on the floor of the train, hemmed in by the seats in a pool of his own excrement, his face locked in a frozen grimace, his body twitching with repeated spasms. The posse of on-lookers had grown, and soon the whole carriage stood around - at a safe distance. All seemed transfixed, unable to utter a word, petrified by the scene of human suffering playing out at their feet. The smell was unbearable. Not the kind of situation Circle participants were accustomed to in their daily life. Karl, ashen, had a look of profound shock in his eyes, as if he were witnessing the scene in complete disbelief.

'Has anyone called the police?' Olena asked as the train pulled into Landquart station.

Day 2

Sunday 14 January 2024
Davos

This morning, the mood at the Circle's subterranean Davos GHQ was sombre and even more tense than usual for the day before the big opening. But then, there was nothing usual about today. Shifting into Emergency Operation Centre mode, the early morning senior staff meeting had been restricted to just four: the boss – known as the Don; Sandra Smily, the forty-something, unflappable American chief communication officer; Phillip Tiddlethwait, the Don's young, urbane British chief of staff; and Markus Bern, the greying Swiss former police officer, who now looked after security at the Circle.

An inauspicious, and painful, start to the Circle's most important week of the year. It had been there before, and now once again, the Circle was in full crisis mode. Damage-limitation deployment. At times like these, the Don could not rely on any of his senior colleagues. He was alone, surrounded by a mixture of yes men and a mutinous crowd of young employees who did as they pleased. A year ago, to the very day, the Defender - the British broadsheet - had put its probing, freedom-of-the press finger on it: "Mutiny erupts among staff". The overtly critical article had infuriated him, but deep down the Don feared that it was perhaps spot on. Good journalism, for sure. It described him as unaccountable to anyone. So what? For God's sake - he'd founded the Circle more than fifty years ago! It was his, and he could run it any bloody way he wanted… couldn't he? The Circle portrayed as a fiefdom, and the managing board as a joke. Maybe! Yes, he was reaching a venerable age this year, but was it his fault that it had always proved so difficult to find a successor? He'd tried years ago with some but had made their life so impossible that they'd all fled. Now he'd given up, appointing instead mediocre, unthreatening seconds who'd never question his decisions and never go very far. No doubt the Circle had become a viper's nest. Politics, in the nastiest possible sense of the word, reigned supreme. But hey: divide and rule! He'd put some hope in a bunch of young professionals pompously called "The Circle Aspiring Leaders", but upon reflexion, they were a mixed blessing. Bright and sharp, but sharks. Zero loyalty. Working at the Circle only for themselves, without giving a toss about the 'mission'. Effective yes, but deeply cynical about the Don and the organisation. He'd let the fox into the henhouse and had only himself to blame, increasingly aware of how much they despised him. He knew they'd be ready to stab him in the back if given a chance, so he never kept them around for too long. Whatever… a sad situation. He couldn't trust anyone. At the first sign of weakness, he'd lose control. Everybody would be at everybody else's throat. So, at times like this, better focus on the matter at hand and limit the number of meeting participants to the strictest minimum – the inner circle of the Circle, so to speak. An expedient way of governing.

'Not a word', uttered the Don. 'We're less than 48 hours from the official opening. We can't allow an unfortunate accident to ruin things. I don't want anybody to discuss this, internally or externally.'

The Don wasn't in a good place this morning. His habit of compulsively pinching his lower lip was the giveaway, an unmistakable sign that he was annoyed or couldn't make up his mind. Or both. The two went hand in hand: the more annoyed he was, the more indecisive he became, and vice versa.

He turned to Markus, and asked sternly:

'How did this happen? What, if anything, does it have to do with us?'

By 'us' he meant the Circle. His baby. His creature. The love of his life.

'We don't know sir. Not yet."

The use of 'sir' didn't go unnoticed. Always appreciated. Not very modern, but a sign of respect and deference that he liked, needed. It still grated when colleagues called him by his first name.

'What did your former colleagues tell you?'

Bern had spent decades in the Swiss gendarmerie before taking early retirement and moving to The Circle as head of security. His job was to make sure that the Swiss police and army knew ahead of time who was expected in Davos, how they were travelling, where they were staying and so on. He also ran The Circle's own security team within the conference centre, made up of other ex-policemen who padded invisibly around the lounges and corridors just in case they were needed, which they rarely were.

Not overly demanding. Easy. Ineffectual. But he was the person whom the Swiss police called when something was up, he'd been one of them. It meant good contacts and the occasional snippets of relevant information.

'The man who died last night after falling ill on the train was Alain Girard. A French independent journalist and author. Said to be known for writing a lot on Russia and Putin, and...'

'Who'd invited him?' interrupted the Don.

'Nobody. Which is to say not us. He was on his way to Davos, but not as our guest. He was going to hang around, interview anyone who'd agree to talk to him.'

'I see…' said the Don, bristling. He couldn't stand the idea of this mass of uninvited opportunists storming the valley and doing business, freeriding on the Circle's hard-won prestige.

'Could it be an accident?' he asked.

'It could be. The results of the autopsy will be known tonight, or tomorrow morning at the latest. I'm told he was diabetic and had a heart condition, so natural causes can't be ruled out. But my contacts say this looks very much like a poisoning.'

The Don turned to Sandra.

'Let's leave the media out of this.'

The regal 'us', by which he meant it was down to Sandra to deal with the situation. Talking to the press had never been his thing. In his mind, journalists equated to vultures always circling ready to scavenge any morsels from his private life and or that of the Circle to get a good story. On a few occasions, he'd been an inch away from a PR disaster. He'd learnt his lesson, and now steered clear.

'I'll do my best sir, but as you know, this is beyond my control.'

'If the proverbial shit does hit the fan, and it is an assassination, we'll always have the option to state that he's not one of our guests', observed Phillip, cannily. 'We did not invite him. We've never heard of him, and we weren't even aware of his presence. This has nothing to do with the Circle.'

Reasonable. Deflecting the responsibility to others. A language the Don liked.

Telling Sandra and Markus they could go, he turned to Phillip.

'Phillip: can you stay behind for one second please?'

'Certainly sir!'

He liked the young Englishman, as much as he liked anybody. A Circle aspiring leader, with all the pre-requisite qualities. Sharp. Hard working. But above all respectful and, as far as he could tell, trustworthy. With Phillip he could talk. Highly recommended by the CEO of a leading British bank - an old 'friend' of the Circle. A safe bet.

*****

The church bell rang four in the afternoon. A soothing, crystalline sound. Olena and Phillip were walking along the Promenade, in the direction of the lake. A moment of insouciance, time suspended. To catch up. They hadn't seen each other for almost three years.

'You haven't changed Olia.'

This time, she didn't mind the affectionate diminutive. Quite the opposite. 'Nor have you!'

'You're as gorgeous and radiant as ever.'

She smiled at him and said nothing. She thought he hadn't changed either. Confident, handsome. She kept that to herself.

'Well done for your new job', he added. 'To head the "Reconstruct Ukraine" fund, this is a monumental task, and daunting. But landing the job at your age is incredible! You must be delighted, and just a little bit proud, no?'

'I'm not sure I deserve congratulations! Had I known it would be this tough, I would have stayed at the Circle. Like you. So much easier. So innocuous. So comfortable.'

Before being appointed by Zelenskyy a year after his election, Olenka had been a Circle employee, one of these bright young "Circle Aspiring Leaders". Two years of schmoozing and networking during which she had relentlessly worked on her own 'rolodex'. But, like her peers, she'd always held the organization in low esteem, incensed by the sense of importance and self-satisfaction that infused it. So full of it!

'And you Phillip? Why are you still there?' she asked, glancing at him. They'd started at the same time, part of the same cohort of "Aspiring Circle Leaders", back in 2017. She'd come from finance – an investment boutique based in New York and Kiev; and he from the British civil service – the Downing Street Policy Unit where he'd gone straight after graduating from Oxford.

'I like the job. It's the only one worth having at the Circle. You know how it works here. I see everything. I hear everything. Fantastic training! And great fun, provided I don't do it for too long.'

She didn't believe a word, certain there was something else. Otherwise, what could have compelled him to work as a lackey to the Don? Something didn't add up. Phillip was much too clever and ambitious for that.

They walked in silence for a while, each privately reminiscing about the affair they had had for a short spell when she lived in Geneva. Phillip broke the silence first.

'We were a great fit you and I.'

Olia looked at him, smiled, and said:

'Were we? We had a lot of fun and a lot of sex. Not much else that I can recall.'

'I was in love with you, but you were not in love with me. That was the problem… Asymmetry! We were not destined to go very far…'

'True', she stated matter-of-factly, before changing the subject.

'How is the Don?'

'Always chasing after something. Obsessed about his legacy! Otherwise, busier than ever and worried, as always. You know him! He's on a mission, reinventing the organisation ten times a year, perpetually concerned that something might go wrong. By the way, did you hear about what happened on the train from Zurich yesterday?'

'Did I hear?' she interrupted, looking at him in disbelief. 'I was in the f…ing carriage!'

Phillip showed genuine astonishment, while concealing genuine interest. 'Incredible! Tell me then! What did you see? What did you learn? What happened? All I know is what I heard on the radio.'

'The French journalist and I were travelling in the same carriage. We vaguely knew each other. He came up uninvited to talk to me, to ask a silly question about Zelenskyy… He wanted more but I made it clear there was no interview to be had. We barely spoke. I didn't like him and am always very wary of that kind of guy. He did sit down opposite me for a few minutes, but then returned to his seat where just moments later he was writhing in agony.'

She paused and risked a joke. 'It wasn't me. I have witnesses.'

'Never thought it for a moment. But you knew him, and you didn't like him?'

'Of course no one deserves that, but he was a snake who worked for Putin. You can be certain of that.'

'Really?

'Yes, really. He was on the take.'

'What makes you so sure?'

'Just Google him. You'll see, he's been one of Putin's puppets for years. He tried to look impartial but was known for recently publishing a series of articles that portray the Russian leadership in a positive light. Three years ago, just before the war, he wrote a book called "We Need Russia" in which he argued that Europe could never prosper without Russia. He interviewed Putin for it, plus several Russian oligarchs.'

'Wow', observed Phillip with an expression of disbelief, as if this were something of a scoop.

'There is more', pursued Olenka. 'He got an offshore payment of a million euros for the book, from an oligarch close to Putin.'

'How do you know that?'

'Because it's been made public in the Cyprus Confidential files. You see …', she said, stopping on the pavement and staring at Phillip, intently.

'… We shouldn't be surprised. This sort of stuff happens all the time, and it's not just the Russians. Others, like the Chinese, are at it as well. All very good at recruiting politicians and journalists, mostly from the far-right, as 'intelligence assets.' Think Frank Creyelman, the Belgian politician who worked for the Chinese for a few years, benefiting from their largesse. Same thing with Alain Girard, but this time on the Russian side. The money he got resembles some kind of sponsorship, but with no strings attached. It's an upfront payment if you like. You receive it and then you are expected to do what you must: sow confusion and division. There are hundreds such people in the West, and you find them everywhere: in business, the media, academia, thinktanks, politics. They form the legions of "useful idiots" employed by Putin and other autocrats, doing the undermining from within for them, eroding our democratic edifice one brick at a time.'

'Sure! We all know that. But I didn't have a clue about this French guy… To be frank and strictly between us, we discussed it this morning with the Don, wondering whether it was just an unfortunate accident. Considering what you just said, an assassination looks far more likely than natural causes…'

'Of course,' Olena said, only just containing the shake in her voice.

She fought off the tears coming to her eyes. Like some other witnesses in the carriage, she'd been briefly questioned by the police in Landquart and asked to give a statement. As a result, she missed her connection for Davos.

The episode had sown the seeds of doubt in her mind. The police seemed to be taking this seriously. But they would, wouldn't they, occurring as it had on the eve of the infamous yearly gathering of the Circle! So? Had Alain Girard died tragically of natural causes, or had he been eliminated? She could think of plenty of reasons why the Russians might want to get rid of him. After all, there had been several such occurrences in the past, in the UK, Bulgaria and elsewhere. She knew they had no qualms about using such methods. A person upsets the regime a bit too much, gets too close to oligarchs X and Y who have fallen from favour with the big boss, or simply ceases to be useful. Such people are expendable, throwaway like a basic commodity. End of story. Olena understood these things. And the more she thought about it, the greater the doubt. Her protective outer layer of self-rationalization was wearing thin. What if this wasn't about the French man at all, but about her? The poisoning! What if she'd been the real target, missed? She recalled the muddle with the various cups of coffee bought at the Starbucks in Zurich station and others from the trolley on the train. Girard mistaking his cup for hers. There had been lots of toing and froing in the carriage, people coming and going, sitting down, getting up. She was confused and could no longer remember or visualize what had actually happened. Had Girard drunk a cup of 'coffee' destined for her?

'I am going back to the hotel now', she said without looking at Phillip.

'Wait!' He shouted before scribbling something on a piece of paper.

'Take this. It's my personal number you can use if you need me urgently. Better than WhatsApp or my Circle number. Send me a message on Signal.' His voice lowered to a whisper. 'You do trust me Olia, don't you?'

'Of course I do!' She smiled. A broad, radiant, confident smile.

All very mysterious! What was he up to?

She kissed him on the cheek, squeezed his hand, turned around and took a few steps. A wave of strange emotions washed over her. A mix of excitement, determination, un-easiness, and anxiety. She inhaled the clear, crisp mountain air and looked up at the sky, ablaze with another beguiling sunset. Billowing orange and violet clouds scudded in front of the darkening peaks. Majestic and mysteriously calm.

Coming from somewhere beyond the clouds, indistinct in the glow of the setting sun, Olena discerned the unmistak-able rhythmic humming of a helicopter. It passed over her, very close. Too close, she thought. It was also lurching from side to side like an injured animal trying to regain its balance. Then, suddenly, a fireball lit up the still glowing dusk with a blood curdling clash of exploding metal. The helicopter had crashed, close to the landing pad.

Day 3

Monday 15 January 2024

Davos

D-day had dawned. The biggest day of the year! The only day that really mattered at the Circle: the opening day of the annual meeting in Davos. The once-a-year opportunity to garner global attention, and above all to celebrate the Don's achievement. And his unrivalled influence: shaking hands with 3,000 among the most powerful, renowned, people on earth. Making history! In his naivety, the Don had always believed that the conversations held in Davos contributed to the course of history. They didn't. Unbeknownst to the Don, money, and the influence it bought, was all that was ever made backstage at the annual meeting.

Who cared?

Let the festivities begin!

But all night the bad news had just kept coming, threatening to spoil everything. It felt like a rain-swollen river about to sweep away twelve months of hard work. First, the shocking revelation that Alain Girard had indeed been poisoned. Then, the seemingly unexplained helicopter crash. And last, the relentless media requests for official comments and interviews with any employee of the Circle who'd dare to speak and shed some light on what was going on. Always the same question: would the tragedy at the helipad compel the organisers to cancel this year's edition? The public did not know about Alain Girard. Yet… Sandra thought it was only a matter of hours before a newspaper or a blogger ran with the scoop. The Don was at his wits' end, having barely slept and spent the night picking the brain of anyone he knew who'd have an opinion to share about what to do next. As so often when confronted with a tough decision, the last to speak to him would be the one to get his ear. At four that morning on a Zoom call, the American CEO of a crisis communication boutique and close adviser for many years convinced him to go ahead no matter what. He knew what the Don wanted to hear, no risk of ever laying it on too thick. He put it just right: 'Your mission is much too important for the world. You can't abandon now. In these troubled times, the Circle is more essential than ever. The world needs to hear what you have to say, and the show must go on'. The word 'show' made the Don wince (the Circle was far too serious an affair to be compared to a show), but he liked the rest. Yes! What he and the Circle were doing was much too important to cancel. The American CEO had offered to draft a communiqué explaining why this year's meeting would go ahead – "a very difficult decision considering the recent, tragic circumstances", but blah blah blah. The Circle had seen it all before and would forge ahead, business as usual. Onwards and upwards!

That morning, the staff meeting was an unusually grim gathering, veiled in pomposity. The meeting room located in the bowels of the Congress Centre had been renamed 'situation room' for the occasion. Two private security agents were posted at the door, not sure of what they were doing there considering that hundreds of police and military forces stood outside, plus their colleagues scanning everybody at the entrance of the building before letting them in. But again: this was no ordinary day. The Don began:

'In light of recent events, I've instructed a small team led by Phillip, assisted by Markus, to be on 24-hour alert. This is to ensure that this year's meeting runs as smoothly as ever. Phillip will report directly to me.'

Succinct and to the point. Within the room, expressions were grave, the demeanour serious. A few managing board members stared at the ceiling, imbued with an inordinate sense of their own importance. They were after all in the "situation room", and thus party to the highly consequential decision about to be taken! Everybody else – Markus, Sandra, Phillip plus a few hangers on from the upper ranks of the organisation – knew what this was all about. All were there to ensure that the senior leadership of the Circle understood and towed to the party line, speaking with one voice. That is, the voice of the Don who stood silent at the end of the table, sombre and reflective. He turned to Markus. His voice was cavernous with an injunctive tone.

'The latest information please!'

'I was in Chur very early this morning for a meeting with the head of the Graubünden cantonal police. There is no doubt whatsoever. The French journalist was poisoned with an organophosphate nerve agent. Something like the substance used by operatives of the GRU, the Russian Military Intelligence, in the UK in 2018, and in other places since', he added with a knowing look. 'It seems the symptoms occurred within hours, or even minutes, due to acute exposure.'

The Don pinched his lower lip hard between his thumb and forefinger, looking hesitant, uneasy.

'And is there any danger for us?'

He corrected himself immediately.

'I mean of course… For our participants?'

'Not that I know of' replied Markus. 'The nerve agent could have been smeared on anything. A door handle, a cup of coffee. Or infused in a drink. For the moment, no traces have been found on the train, but the police are only at the beginning of their investigation. It's in the hands of the forensic unit. It will take a little while.'

An apocalyptic image flashed through the Don's mind: the police clad from top to toe in full hazmat gear, searching for clues in the carriage. In Landquart. Just a stone's throw away from Davos. That would be the *coup de grace*. The media would have a field day. He looked at Sandra, composed.

'Do whatever is needed to prevent photos from being taken and published, please.'

She stared at him, incredulous.

'I'll do my best sir.'

He turned to Markus again.

'And the helicopter: what happened?'

'An incredible, inexplicable accident… The pilot had thousands of flight hours. He'd done Zurich-Davos hundreds of times. It seems that he approached the landing pad in a bizarre manner. As he was about to land, he regained a few meters, veered to the left and this is when the blades clipped a cable or a mast… or a building. We are not one hundred per cent sure yet. The police are investigating.'

'We are naturally saying this is an accident', interjected Sandra with a false air of conviction.

'Let's hope so', observed Markus. 'The radar that followed the flight up the valley shows at times an unusual trajectory, as if the pilot were under the influence - alcohol or drugs. I'll hear about the results of the autopsy tomorrow.'

The Don stared at everybody around the table with an intense look. 'It is surely an accident', he said. 'It cannot be otherwise.'

'Let's hope so', Markus repeated. Undaunted, he went on to distribute a small, printed note. 'Here are the names of the deceased' he explained.

No secrets here - everybody knew already. Together with the pilot, four others had died, all Circle invitees, all white badges.

'So', continued Markus, 'what we know is that the American hedge fund manager had hosted a lunchtime reception at the Hotel Baur du Lac in Zurich to celebrate the launch of a new charity. About 50 in total. I have that list too. It seems that after lunch he invited whoever wanted to go with him to share his chartered helicopter to Davos because he had three spare seats. We don't know who volunteered and how the final choice of passengers was made, but what we do know', he went on to explain in his heavily accentuated German accent, 'is that a French academic known for his work on inequalities, a young British socialite, activist and philanthropist, and a journalist from Ukraine were on board the helicopter. They are all dead.'

The Don stared at each person seated around the table, one by one, with an authoritative look that verged on the threatening.

'We'll proceed with the annual meeting. Any questions?'

They surveyed each other in silence, pondering whether anyone in the room would dare to ask one, let alone object to the decision. The customary awkwardness. Not great for self-esteem, but everybody knew the rota. Phillip's mind was elsewhere. One of his phones had been vibrating several times. He discreetly glanced at the screen below the edge of the table. A notification on Signal. Unusual. He thought he knew who it was from. He clicked on the message. 'meet at the top of seehorn. 1am tonight. Have the evidence'. Slightly higher than 2,200 metres the Seehorn was a modest mountain by Alpine standards, and just outside Davos. But even so, getting to the top of it would mean a 500-metre ascent on skis, in the middle of the night, in the middle of nowhere. Not a problem in itself for a skier of Phillip's experience, but why so late? Why on top of a mountain? Why not in a more accessible location?

He typed hastily. 'why there? Are you out of your mind?' and hit the arrow. A response came back immediately. 'discretion is of the essence', accompanied by a smiling emoji.

*****

Late that evening, after making himself briefly conspicuous at the opening reception, Phillip returned to his small apartment in Talstrasse. He took his time to prepare eve rything in the warmth and relative comfort of the studio. He was calm, in control and meticulous. First, he placed a waterproof case in the top pocket of his backpack. He'd need that later. In the main pocket he then stowed an extra layer of clothing, a snack, and a flask of tea. He strapped on his ice-axe, then reached under his bed and pulled out the lockbox containing his gun, a Glock 19. He put the firearm into its holster strapped to his chest, just inside his hooded goretex ski jacket. If needed, he could remove his ski gloves and fire it in less than three seconds. For good measure, he added two extra magazines of 15 rounds in each of the outside pockets. The message on Signal hadn't dented his confidence, but better safe than sorry, he thought while setting aside his avalanche transceiver. On an icy cold night, the risk of avalanche was almost nil. And anyway, he was on his own and nobody was going to come to his rescue. He stuck the velvety 'skins' to his skis, adjusted his head lamp on his close-fitting hat, zipped up his jacket and went outside. He was in great shape and confident it would only take him about an hour and a bit to reach the top of the mountain. It was half past eleven and freezing cold.

Once in the snow-covered courtyard, he put his skis on straightaway, like the locals, and turned into Bündastrasse before reaching a little footpath buried in the snow. It took him less than ten minutes to get to the Flüelastrasse, deserted at that time of night, cross it, and start his ascent. He hadn't seen a soul. He was alone, in the splendid solitude of the moonlit mountain. At this altitude, the night was clear and silent. His skis slid with scarcely a sound. The snow was icy, making his progress almost easy. He switched off his head lamp and soon found his rhythm. He'd be at the top of Seehorn well before 1am.

In this glacial, hypnotic desert whose impeccable whiteness reverberated in the darkness of the night, he felt serene, almost free. Occasionally, snow flurries unleashed by the wind wiped everything from view. The contours of the slope, the mountain range in the distance - everything became indistinct, and at times he could barely even distinguish the shapes of the ridges. Not a problem. He was just focused on his effort and the task of putting one ski in front of the other, and again, forward, and upward. He knew what he was doing, was at ease. As he climbed, his lungs felt the metallic coldness of the mountain air. The summit must be getting closer, but as the weather closed in, the snow flurries grew thicker and the wind increasingly violent. He could not make out the dome of Seehorn. Only the majestic mountains in the distance, and the lights of the valley and its secrets below, were still just visible. As a patch of freezing fog suddenly rolled in, slowly, inexplicably, a sliver of suspicion entered his mind. An inner voice called for caution. He checked his watch. The altimeter indicated 2,170 metres. Fifty more to go. He had time in hand and that gave him an idea. Any person at the top would expect him to arrive from the south, but instead of reaching the Seehorn by the normal route, he would reach the summit by the north-west, on a much steeper slope. He put his ski crampons on, took the ice axe from his backpack and started the conversions on the vertiginous tongue of ice, turning every ten meters or so.

He was almost at the top, when, between two gusts of wind, he heard voices conversing agitatedly. Three or four – he wasn't sure. How come? Who was there? He stopped in his tracks, suspended on the sharp gradient of the slope. He was close, very close, maybe only two conversions away from the summit. He couldn't see them; they couldn't see him – the 40-degree slope was just too steep. Focused on the depth of his own breathing, Phillip made a snap decision. He'd need at least a minute to remove the skins before he could ski down. Balancing in the void with the help of his ice axe, he took off his skis, and ripped the skins from them, as quietly as he could. Next, he put his skis back down, forcing their edges into the snow to make sure he didn't lose them. Carefully, holding onto the axe, he inserted his left ski boot in the binding, triggering a metallic thud. Then the right one. Another thud. Suddenly, the voices at the top went silent. They'd heard. He abandoned his axe, grabbed his ski poles, and pivoting on them, he made a sharp turn, plunging into the void just before the crackle of automatic gunfire. Dozens of bullets flew around him, splintering shards of ice into the night sky.

Phillip disappeared into the darkness.

Day 4

Tuesday 16 January 2024

Davos

The Don stared into his emerald, green multivitamin morning drink in a bid to control the mounting maelstrom in his mind. He couldn't think straight, couldn't hold a thought, only one kept recurring – that this could be the end of it all. His crowning achievement, what he'd laboured for his entire life, was at risk of unravelling in a matter of hours before his very eyes.

Five deaths in two days, the sinister news about the helicopter pilot, and now Phillip nowhere to be found. The last straw – incomprehensible. His disappearance defied imagination! How could his chief of staff vanish into thin air just when he needed him the most, two days into the world's most important gathering?! What was he up to? Phillip had failed to show up at the 6 am senior staff meeting, and nobody had the faintest idea why or where he might be. It was now 10am. For three hours, rescue police dogs had scoured the snow-clad streets of Davos in vain, while the search for clues in and around Phillip's studio had yielded nothing but his professional mobile left on the bedside table. He'd simply evaporated. How could this have happened in what was at this particular moment, the most surveilled place on earth? Gradually, like a seeping poison, a sense of panic gripped the Don. It was the same for the trusted few who had seen Phillip's empty chair. All morning, he'd kept shouting: 'Not a word, not a message on social media, nothing. Nothing!' But for how long could the news of Phillip's disappearance be kept under wraps? A question to be resolved later. Pressing but not the priority. There was already more than enough on the Circle's plate that morning.

In Davos, it was kind of business-as-usual. Participants sashayed through the corridors of the congress centre and the opportunistically over-priced hotel lobbies and restaurants in town. Doing business, closing deals. It felt almost normal. Yet the atmosphere was charged. Rumours about the helicopter crash and the journalist's death had emerged, spreading like wildfire. Virality at work, with myriad conjectures about Alain Girard's death already in circulation. So much so that those looking for an explanation could not dissociate information from misinformation, and misinformation from disinformation. Sometimes, it was the Russians who did it. Sometimes the Americans. Sometimes, someone else. Who knew? Similarly competing conspiracy theories circulated about the helicopter crash, even though nobody knew yet about the pilot's condition. But it would only be a matter of hours, maybe a day, before the news leaked that he was flying under the influence. For now, only the Don knew, informed by Markus earlier that day. The helicopter stories were centred on a supposed sabotage aimed at eliminating the Ukrainian investigative journalist or the British socialite and philanthropist, now known to be Rebecca Stilton. She was a regular at the Circle and had supposedly come this year to promote the "Anything but Trump" initiative. This revelation had enraged the Don. Furious, he'd quickly summoned Markus for a one-to-one.

'Why didn't we know anything about this group? I would never have authorized it. This could put our impartiality at risk!'

'I conducted a quick investigation,' began the head of security, flipping through the pages of a notebook, 'and my conclusion is that some of this year's participants are here to discuss how to prevent Trump's re-election by any means possible. This English lady seemed to be one of them, but there must be others here in Davos. We don't know exactly who they are, we only know it's an international group. Individuals so afraid of a Trump victory and its consequences that they'll stop at nothing to prevent it from happening.'

A few seconds passed. The Don was livid. A cold, inner anger.

'What do you mean by "any means possible" and "stop at nothing"? And who gave you this information?'

'I don't know what sort of means they have in mind, sir. My contacts in the Swiss government shared this information with me. But it remains very vague. Details about this organisation, or initiative, or whatever it is, are sparse. They don't have a website, there is no publicity, nothing is public. I just know that quite a few high-level individuals from several Western countries are involved and that some of them are here in Davos this week.'

The Don thumped the table with a clenched fist.

'How dare they?' he shouted. 'We are not a political party, or an activist movement. I don't want this sort of thing taking place at the Circle, you understand? We are not here to take position against this or that. Our neutrality is our *raison d'être*, our strength! Please find out who these people are. I want to make sure they don't use our name or platform to advance their agenda.'

'I understand. Thank you, sir.'

Imprisoned by all the contradictions that had defined his career, the Don stared at the wall with an absent gaze. What to make of this? What could he do? His meeting with Trump, a few years back, had left a bitter taste in his mouth. Not because he'd shared the stage with such an unsavoury character, but rather because of what had followed: accusations that he'd been much too deferential, even sycophantic, to the controversial US president. Sure, he'd praised him for his leadership and inclusiveness, but why not? Or was "inclusiveness" going a bit too far? An overstep? Absolutely not! He'd always maintained a pleasant and respectful stance when engaging with world leaders, be they autocrats or democrats, sanguinary or benevolent. The Don had intended The Circle to be above ideologies, but now there was no above. The world seemed to have subordinated everything to ideologies. Even so, who was he to stand in judgement? For sure, not every guest in Davos was morally wholesome, but having them around was the price to pay if you were committed to making the world a better place, wasn't it?

*****

At around the same time, Olena was labouring her way through back-to-back meetings in the Hotel Belvedere, the most coveted venue in town. Karl Manhof had a suite there, which he'd suggested as the best possible location for their ongoing negotiations.

'You see Olenka: smart but discrete. That's what you need to impress all the civil servants!'

The arrogance of the man. An unbearable sense of entitlement pervaded everything he did, said and was. But she acquiesced. After all, he had the money. And he'd insisted on being present at every single meeting she'd have in Davos. Therefore, she needed him on her side. Him and his money.

They'd spent most of the day negotiating different projects with delegations from countries and organisations committed to taking part in Ukraine's reconstruction. Always the same pitch. Always the same promise from Karl to match public money with private capital. Always the same emphasis on greening the reconstruction of Ukraine, and always the same pledges from their counterparts. 'We'll look at this with utmost interest.' 'We won't let you down'. 'Ukraine's future is our future'. An overload of utter banalities and barely any time to draw breath. It was past 6pm. Their last meeting for that day had just left the suite.

Olena stood up, stretched, and exhaling somewhat theatrically, said in an exasperated voice:

'My verdict for the day: long on promises, short on substance.'

'That's a bit harsh!'

She'd heard that one before.

'Let's face it, Karl. Ukraine has already lost 50 per cent of its generation capacity because of the war. Here in Davos, we are talking about rebuilding our energy sector in a green, sustainable, manner. Do you think many of our partners are going to buy into this when the situation on the ground is so grim?'

Then she added, pointing her finger at the German billionaire:

'Now that the US and you Europeans are cutting back your aide and military assistance to my country, who is going to be mad enough to invest at all, let alone in a "green and sustainable manner"? This wavering of support wields a potentially fatal blow to Ukraine, but you can be sure we will not be the only ones to pay – in the long run it will cost you, the democratic West, very dearly too. Tell me: who are we kidding with all this?'

'Listen', argued Karl with his customary, unflagging optimism, 'nothing's decided. I don't think the West will let you down. And this afternoon the three Americans seemed pretty keen. The proof will be in the pudding!' he added with his annoying self-satisfied smile.

'Keen on pledges, for sure. They cost nothing. My president will be here in two days for the closing. Not official yet, but I'm sure he'll come. Am I going to present pledges or commitments to him? I need signed agreements! That's what I need Karl.'

'Patience!' smiled Karl. 'Two days is a long time in Davos. You will see twenty more people tomorrow, all of them with something to offer. You'll get your signed agreements. We both know the EU. It will take an age, but it will come through in the end. As for the US, the chap from USAID and the Democrat from Congress just promised to get back to us with a Memorandum of Understanding by tomorrow night.'

She stared at him with an air of disbelief. Over the past two days, some discussions she'd had with a few academics and policymakers she knew and whose opinion she valued had given rise to a profound sense of foreboding. They'd all argued the world was becoming much messier, inexorably. A slow burn punctuated by occasional major crises like her country's war with Russia, Israel and Hamas, Sudan, Nagorno-Karabakh and many others. And maybe China and the US before too long? She knew they were right. Her morale had taken a beating, and she was now fixated on the idea that a Trump victory in November would turbocharge this descent into global chaos. The first major casualty after his election? Her country of course, and her project. Deeply pessimistic thoughts, but nothing she had heard so far at this year's gathering could dispel them. The optimists' comforting conviction that the world would be all right rested on a secure foundation: their unlimited capacity to fool themselves. Like for Trump. In 2016, when she was a junior employee in an investment fund in NYC, it had seemed inconceivable that someone like Trump could be elected. And then he was. Then in 2020, it seemed just unimaginable that an American president would try to remain in office after losing an election. But he did. In 2023, it seemed unconscionable that Trump, having failed to invalidate the election, would reemerge as the unchallenged leader of the Republican party. Yet he had. 2024? She was confident he'd become its nominee again, and win. Barring a miracle, it was a done deal.

'I've written off the US', she said before adding: 'The odds of a Trump victory and the country falling into a dictatorship next year are not insignificant. And even if dictatorship doesn't happen, we are fucked. No more NATO, no more this, no more that. Donald will cuddle up to his friend Vladimir, and Ukraine will foot the bill.'

Karl responded lamely:

'Come on Olenka! It's not all gloom and doom. Nothing is pre-ordained'.

She shook her head in resigned disagreement and glanced at her watch. 6.45pm.

'Let's call it a day. The nice US democrat whom we met earlier has asked me to join him and his wife for a drink.'

'There, you see: things aren't as bad as all that!'

*****

She gathered her stuff and hastily scrolled through her email and messages. She hadn't had two minutes during the day to do so. Hundreds were waiting, unopened. She glanced at them, quickly. Several WhatsApp from former Circle colleagues in Davos asking her whether she knew anything about Phillip. Apparently, he'd gone awol and nobody knew where he was. "The plot thickens at this year's Davos", said one, adding: "Could this be a chain reaction? What's the connecting link?" She didn't like that and shivered, despite the insufferable heat in the hotel. Was that a premonition? She took her puffer jacket from the coat rack, and rummaging in the pockets, found what she was looking for: the number Phillip had given her three days earlier. 6.50pm. She couldn't be late for the Congressman, but she needed to reassure herself. She quickly installed the Signal app that she'd never used before then typed: "p: how are you and where are you? please respond. olia". She sent it and hurried downstairs.

The lobby was packed. She made her way out among dozens of Circle participants about to leave for dinner. A fleet of luxury cars waited for them in the icy courtyard. No more than a few metres separated the entrance steps from the cars approaching one by one under the supervision of security guards, yet the vast majority of the diners, in the name of prudence, had opted to wear unfamiliar mini crampons to affront this meagre expanse of "Arctic ice pack" The result: looking comically penguin-like they waddled rhythmically to their limos. Beyond the 'colony', Olena spotted the Congressman, his wife by his side. She went over to them and shook their hands.

'How very nice to see you again and to meet you Madame...'

'The pleasure is mine, Ms. Kostarenko. Where shall we go? Do you have a favourite place in Davos?'

She looked at him and liked him. The same feeling as in the meeting earlier: he inspired confidence.

If it would suit you both, let me suggest that we stay here in the Belvedere and ...

She didn't have time to add another word. As if in slow motion, a moment suspended in time, she saw the bullet entering the Congressman's temple and exiting the other side. His head exploded, and in a gruesome shower of blood and bones he collapsed before Olena. Glass shattered somewhere nearby. Then the Senator`s wife screamed in terror. Olena screamed too.

*****

Less than half an hour later, Olena was alone in her room at the Schweizerhof with a police officer positioned outside her door. The police had driven her there, verified her identity while she was still in the car and asked her why she'd met with the Congressman. After she'd struggled to put a few sentences together she was accompanied to her room and invited to rest. A nurse would be with her shortly. The police would talk to her again when the shock had passed. And, in the meantime, if she remembered anything about those moments just before the shooting, she should write them down. They gave her a notepad and ballpoint. They then left, leaving her alone. She collapsed on to the sofa, ignoring repeated phone calls from the Don and other former colleagues at the Circle. Through the door, she could hear the police officer whispering in Swiss German. But what difference would that make if they were after her? If she was the target, hundreds, if not thousands, of police and army forces deployed in Davos and its surroundings were just an irrelevance.

But was she? Her first instinct was to reach out to Phil. She opened Signal. He had replied.

'i'm fine olia, but you won't see me for the rest of the week. take good care of yourself'. Sent at 6.52pm, immediately after she'd sent hers.

With trembling fingers, she typed: '"man shot next to me just now. congressman. need advice. please help" and tapped the arrow.

Phillip shot back almost immediately.

'presume you now in hotel and police with you. if so, go nowhere and do nothing. wait 'til i tell you what to do next.'

'why? who are you, phil? i mean, for real?'

'my business is to know what others don't. Please olia trust me. you know you can. i'll get back to you.'

Then he was gone.

Day 5

Wednesday 17 January 2024
Davos

As unusual nights go, this one was off the scale. By the end of it, all participants knew something was amiss. Seriously amiss.

Many had been drinking into the early hours, engaged in a desperate attempt to make sense of the unexplained series of catastrophes besieging this year's meeting. The peaceful Davos landscape had taken an unusual turn: armoured vehicles criss-crossed the snowy streets, while groups of soldiers in full military gear and heavily armed police patrolled the hotel lobbies and restaurants. Swiss army helicopters cluttered the sky with powerful spotlights sweeping across the mountain, the mournful hum of their blades tearing through the silence of the night.

The evening before, the Don had appealed for calm on the Circle's messaging app, advising the Circle's "distinguished participants" to remain in their hotel rooms. But few cared and even fewer had heeded the advice. Many had gone out, filling restaurants and bars, drinking as if there was no tomorrow, gossiping about the news, in an adrenalin-charged atmosphere, laced with a mix of excitement and apprehension. At 2am, the village was still abuzz with activity. No one could dispute that the Circle hadn't been this interesting for years – but maybe a bit too interesting for some! Behind the buzz and the frenzy, anxiety lurked, even if for the moment the sheeplike reflex of being together, of standing by each other (quite unusual by participants' standards), provided the illusory comfort that in the end everything would be fine.

Or would it?

Most conversations centred on what might happen next, or more precisely who might be next. Was there a serial killer at work? A madman with such grievances against the global elite that he was ready to eliminate a bunch of them in Davos? Or maybe a secret organisation?

Collective imagination ran wild.

The journalist's death and the helicopter crash that had aroused lurid curiosity just 48 hours earlier were now consigned to distant memory. Last night's shootings were a very different kettle of fish. Far too close for comfort. How on earth could two high profile participants, a prominent Democrat Congressman and the CEO of one of the largest American banks, be shot down like rabbits at a 10-second interval in two different parts of town? Unconscionable! The scenario belonged to the exaggerated plot of a second-rate spy novel. Yet it had happened. And it had emerged that these were not conventional hits, so to speak. Barely three hours after the shootings, anybody with an internet connection anywhere in the world could read that both victims had been shot with a 7.62×51mm

NATO round, probably from a considerable distance; one and a half miles or so. What this meant was that these two shootings, most likely planned weeks in advance, were the work of at least four highly trained professionals - two snipers plus a spotter each to make the wind call, all hidden in the mountains at a safe distance from the town centre, right under the nose of some of the world's tightest security procedures.

Information, news, rumours, were moving fast. Too fast for anybody to make sense of them.

*****

What happened next that night focussed minds to a whole different degree. The valley was closed. Yes: all Circle participants, irrespective of their status or influence, were prevented from leaving. Reminiscent of Agatha Christie's house party guests in a remote country house, anyone present in Davos at the time of the killings now had to remain there. So astonishing was this news that at first it was met with incredulity, particularly by those at the very top of the world's pecking order - the politicians, the global CEOs, the central bankers, and others of their ilk.

Who on earth had the authority to order them to stay? To lock them down like common criminals? They were all manically busy, their actions and decisions impacting hundreds of thousands, if not millions, of people. Surely there'd be an exception for them! But no, there were no exceptions. The far-reaching measure was taken less than thirty minutes after the shootings by the Graubünden cantonal police and the Swiss authorities. No justification, no timing given, no arguments brooked.

In the end, most understood, and all had no choice but to accept the situation. Finding the killers and ensuring no other "terrorists" were hiding in the mountains was paramount. Switzerland's reputation and the participants' security were at stake.

Indignation and outrage were soon replaced by a sense of resignation, even among the hundreds unable to return to their hotels in Klosters, ten kilometres down the valley.

A practical issue: Davos had no room available anywhere in town. The residents had flown to rent their flat at an extravagant price to the participants, while all hotels, good and bad, central or not, were chock-a-block. In haste, some organised camp beds in their lobby, restaurant or even outside in the special tents set up for side-events. A few magnanimous CEOs with suites proposed to accommodate their peers in their spare room. Others with twin-bedded rooms offered up their second beds. Amidst the chaos many bad jokes were made. Davos was turned upside down. Yet somehow the feverish atmosphere remained remarkably friendly, almost surreal. Never in the whole history of the Circle had there been such a sense of solidarity. It wouldn't last.

That night, a few mutinous participants tried to outsmart the police, deciding after one-too-many drinks to drive or walk out of the valley. No chance. The Flüela and Wolfgang pass to Klosters were heavily guarded and closed to any kind of traffic – train, car and even skidoos. So was the Albula pass at the other end of the valley.

Others were more daring. Assembled over many beers and schnaps in the Belvedere's Arvenstübli, half a dozen hedge fund managers were plotting to escape by ski-touring over the Strela pass.

'Not a problem' said one bragging about his ultra-trail exploits around his chalet in Verbier. 'We are all super fit. Let's do it guys! And cherry on the cake: I've ordered a limo minivan that will be waiting for us near Klosters. We'll be at Zurich airport by lunchtime.'

A Swiss investor in the group who also happened to be a reserve officer in the Swiss army knew better. He pointed out that this pass would be closed too, like other possible high-altitude routes such as the Sertig and Scaletta passes. All placed under the close surveillance of the Swiss army's mountain troops, and members of the AAD10, the professional elite unit.

Too bad. The exciting escape was abandoned, and another round of schnaps ordered.

*****

That morning, Davos woke with a hangover.

Circle participants emerged from troubled slumbers or monumental binges still hoping that it was all just a bad dream. No: their nightmare was for real. All trapped in

Davos' sumptuous solitude. All unable to tell when this would come to an end.

They slowly gathered in the Congress Centre, having been told the night before via the messaging app that an "important information meeting" would take place there at 9am.

By 8.50am, the plenary room was full. So too the adjacent rooms connected via video to absorb the overflow. The atmosphere was one of an impatient hubbub tending towards explosive. At nine sharp, the Don appeared on stage, gazing at the gigantic space. The fuss slowly subsided. Looking stiffer than usual, and distinctly uncomfortable, he walked to the lectern, followed by a tall, athletic man in his fifties, whom he introduced as Alois Hersli, the high-level official in the Swiss federal government in charge of security at Davos.

'These are troubling times', he started, with a slow, painful allocution, his eyes fixed on the notes.

For someone who'd delivered thousands and thousands of addresses, speaking in public did not come naturally. Lacking oratory skills, he was not to deviate an inch from the speech that an army of crisis communication specialists had finessed for him during the night. Why take the risk of connecting emotionally with the crowd by improvising when conditions were so adverse?

'As you probably all know by now, last night at around 7pm two of our esteemed guests were shot dead here in the streets of Davos. I offer my deepest condolences to their families as, I am sure, we all do.'

He paused for a few seconds, to allow for a sympathetic murmur.

'After these tragic events, the Graubünden cantonal police force, in conjunction with the Swiss authorities, decided to close the valley with immediate effect for a limited period to better proceed with the investigation and hopefully arrest as rapidly as possible the perpetrators of these two abominable, odious crimes. This is of course a decision totally independent of the Circle and over which we have no control. I regret the tremendous inconvenience this causes to all of you, and I beg for your patience and understanding. Sandra, our director of communications, is here to answer any question you may have, but prior to Sandra, Mr. Hersli will say a few words.'

And with that, he left the stage, cowed and confused, beset by sombre thoughts. What the hell was going on? Was there a connection between this disparate set of catastrophes? Was someone intent on destroying the reputation he'd taken decades to build? Why him? Why Davos? And where was Phillip? All these questions and many more assailed his mind, but the inexplicable absence of his chief of staff tormented him the most. The more he thought about it, the less sense it made. Where on earth had he gone?

Alois Hersli uttered a few banalities in broken English. One after the other, he mentioned Alain Girard's poisoning, the helicopter crash, and the previous day's shootings, explaining that each was being thoroughly investigated by the relevant authorities with the full support of Switzerland's allies. He did acknowledge that the perpetrators of the shooting were most certainly highly skilled special forces members, because despite the considerable resources deployed in the valley and the mountains, they hadn't been found yet. He too apologized for the inconvenience, elaborated a bit on the necessity to lock down the valley, raised his head from the lectern, thanked everybody for their patience and turned away.

Among the participants, the camaraderie of the night before had given way to deep sentiments of anxiety combined with anger. Hersli's intervention had done nothing to assuage either, and he exited the plenary room to a concert of boos, shouts, and recriminations. The normally well-behaved group was not its usual self. The world's powerbrokers had turned into a bunch of unruly individuals.

Sandra took her place at the lectern, jumping in at the deep end. Aware of how pointless it was to counter the millions of explanations, rumours and conspiracies pervading social media and the web, she and the Don had decided that 'in the name of transparency' any question would be taken, instantly transcribed on the mega screen behind her. A monumental challenge. Grasping the mike with both hands, she looked hopelessly at the room. Total chaos. Hapless hostesses doing their best, but useless in the face of such collective incivility, people grabbing the microphone from each other, shouting at each other, security agents overwhelmed, communicating feverishly on their two-way radios, running around like headless chickens. From this pandemonium came an incessant burst of questions, each appearing randomly in red letters on the screen, without curation. "Was the Circle aware of the reason why the two men had been killed? Was the Circle involved, in any way or fashion, in what had happened over the past three days? Were other police forces or secret services involved in the investigation? Were the shooters still in the valley? Was it true that all these crimes were related to the impending visit of President Zelenskyy in Davos? Would Zelenskyy nonetheless come tomorrow? Would the Circle bring the meeting to an abrupt end? For how long would they be prevented from leaving Davos? Was it true that the Circle chief of staff had disappeared and had been eliminated?" And so on. Endless. The room was on fire. A few journalists with a white badge were speaking on two or three phones at once, screaming to be heard. The non-stop 'ping' of social media notifications irradiated the room, the sound level amplifying as each tried to out-shout the other. Sandra had no idea where to start, what to do. She'd been thrown to the wolves.

Take the easy one first, she said to herself. I'll improvise for the others.

Summoning her courage, she called for silence, many, many times. The brouhaha slowly died down.

'I want to address first your question regarding the duration of the lockdown, and want to reassure you about the fact...'

Before she could finish her sentence, a man in his fifties burst onto the stage and snatched the mike from her grasp.

'I'm a foreign minister from a country in the global south', he shouted first to the crowd, then turning to Sandra:

'Is it true that the US Secretary of State has already left Davos, together with all the US Congressmen and Senators attending the annual meeting?'

It was. In a major error of judgment, Markus had confided this vital piece of information during the early morning staff meeting. The whole managing board was thus in the know. At about 4am, eight American VIPs had left for greener pastures in two bullet-proofed, road-bombed resistant minivans that the Swiss Federal Intelligence Service always brought to Davos at that time. Just in case…

Sandra hesitated. She couldn't confirm. She couldn't deny. What to do? Her face flushed; her mouth dried up. She was at a complete loss.

Before she could utter a word, the minister looked at the entire room with gravity, in a theatrical way. Waving a clenched fist, he began to shout rhythmically, emphatically:

'Disgrace! Disgrace! Disgrace!'

Then adding for stronger effect:

'Shame on the Circle! Shame on the Circle! Shame on the Circle! One rule for Americans, one rule for everyone else, and no rules at all for the Americans who make the rules! Enough is enough. Is the 95% of the world's population that is not Westerner going to remain subservient to the will of the Americans for ever? And you, my dear fellow Americans in this room, is it right that your officials go free while you are imprisoned here in Davos? Is this what the Circle means by inclusion? Is this what American democracy means? No, ladies and gentlemen of Davos, we won't accept that! We know the world has changed! Who is with me on that one?'

Many stood up – remarkable considering most of the room was distinctly white. The minister kept stirring… He knew he had the sympathy of the group. Everybody was pissed off, and nobody wanted to be cooped up for too long,

'Follow me on to the Promenade! We are going to walk our way out of Davos. We are going to show them who we are, and we shall assert our rights as citizens to move about freely and peaceably. Nothing can stop us! Enough of paternalism and Western colonialism! Enough of the Circle and its smooth talking! Enough of good intentions! Enough of keeping quiet! Let's walk to Klosters in unison!'

A wave of applause engulfed the room.

'One last thing,' cried the newly endorsed Pied Piper. 'Let's all demand that the Circle apologise to us all of us for its moral cowardice, for its double standards, and for its readiness to conspire with the American and Swiss government to imprison its own guests. We meet on the Promenade in one hour!'

Helpless, the Don watched all of this on a monitor from behind the stage. The words about the Circle sounded like the death knell for his illusions. His most painful moment, the unravelling of his *opus.*

The foreign minister had hit the nail on the head: the world has changed, leaving him and his creature in the lurch, and now the whole world would know. He had appointed himself Admiral of a fleet that was sailing away without him, before his very eyes, towards a new world disorder where power would belong to a violent cabal of disparate countries bound to one another only by their common hatred for the remnants of the Western "world order" to which he had devoted his life, and which he had imagined to be eternal. Folly! This world had come to a brutal end. The Don had begun to understand all this, but too late. Listening to the minister's disembodied incendiary diatribe, he realised the Circle had to change. Structurally. Seriously. Not superficially, as before. Hubris taking hold amidst thc hysteria, he dreamt for a fleeting moment that he could work a quick fix. He already had a handful of Asian women on the managing board, with all the other seats in the hands of a club-like group of Western men. Why not get rid of them and fast? Thus, with a single flamboyant gesture, de-westernizing the Circle's top leadership and re-asserting a new legitimacy. This moment of illusory confidence didn't last long. Who could he ask? Who from the global south would now even consider joining the Circle's top leadership after the debacle of the past few days?

The Don was not an emotional man, but at this moment he could have sobbed. From frustration, from anger, from despair.

He knew the writing was on the wall.

*****

The foreign minister left the stage, gesturing to the crowd to follow him.

The plenary room in Davos had on rare occasions in the past seen standing ovations, but none like this. As one, the room rose to its feet and surged towards the exits. It was a stampede by any other name, only this time the herd was made up of 3,000 of the world's most powerful and famous individuals. Olena had been standing at the back of room behind the last row of chairs. She was not among those rushing to leave, since she was hoping to spot Karl, and she had resigned herself to being jostled by the throng. Then she noticed that the man in the chair just in front of her, who had stood up to leave, seemed to be swaying. A lot. He was clutching at the chair in front. He was trying not to fall over.

'Can someone help please? I feel very dizzy…'

She recognised Mark Massover, the young CEO of Carbon Markets Integrity who'd been begging her for a meeting ever since she'd arrived in Davos.

'How can I help you? What's going on?' asked an individual emerging from the *mêlée*.

'I suddenly feel so unwell. I think I'm going to pass out. Could you call a doctor?' he spluttered before falling to the floor.

His head hit the carpet-clad concrete with an ominous thud.

Day 6

Thursday 18 January 2024

Davos

It'd been a short night for Olena. She had spent it lying sleepless in her bed, staring aimlessly at the ceiling, with the events of the past few days coursing feverishly through her mind. Just when, consumed by fatigue, she was on the point of falling asleep, the nightmarish image of the Congressman's smiling face exploding in front of her re-surfaced, banishing any chance of peaceful rest. After a couple more spells of fitful napping, she conceded that she might as well give up the struggle. She looked at her watch. It was 5am. She got up and reached for her laptop.

Overnight, waves of emails had inundated her professional and personal inboxes. Her WhatsApp and LinkedIn accounts were awash with hundreds of messages. She opened Signal. A message from Phil was waiting. "thinking of you. you are safe. i am offline but will msg again later today. p"

She gazed fixedly at the text, as if somehow closer scrutiny might dispel some of the mystery. But her head continued to spin with questions. Why was he so cryptic? What did he mean by 'safe'? Who was he really? What was this other life, and had he always had it, even when they were together? What side was he on? And the most crucial question of all: could she trust him?

She'd respond to him later. For now, she was desperate for an explanation, for any piece of information that could help make sense of this cataclysmic series of events. Above all, she was desperate for anything that could reassure her. She was baffled. Did she a have a leading role in this relentless series of bloody dramas, or was she simply an unfortunate spectator on their periphery? The more she turned things over in her mind, the greater the indecision. She'd been in the wrong place at the wrong time too many times for it to be mere bad luck. The train, the shooting – and there were the other coincidences. Her journalist friend in the helicopter, then yesterday in the packed plenary room, Mark Massover 'choosing' to pass out just in front of her. Yet, she thought, if, for whatever reason, I am the target, I'd already be dead. Where to look for clues? Her first instinct took her to the Circle's unofficial WhatsApp group. Managed by a coterie of former employees feeding off the gossip provided by those still on the inside, it knew how to place the inner workings of the Circle under a microscope, dissecting it with the precision of a scalpel. Sardonic and often damning. She opened it, skimming through an endless feed as fast as she could. Most messages centred on the Don's reaction to the whole drama, his pathological obsession to keep going no matter what. He'd abandoned the situation room, was on his own, consulting from his bunker with God knows who. His ship was caught in a mammoth storm; he conveyed the impression of an exhausted captain plugging leaks with a small bowl.

There were also many messages questioning Phillip's whereabouts and what might be going on, offering various hypotheses to explain the unexplainable. The Don's chief of staff had disappeared, but why and where to? Theories abounded. Had he been sacked by the Don for working multiple jobs, a practice common among almost all Aspiring Circle Leaders? Was he the victim of a major conflict of interest with one of the Circle's partners? All these were plausible scenarios, but none could justify a sacking at such a critical juncture, and in full view at Davos. Was there a hidden agenda? Had he blackmailed the boss? Was he a secret agent? Or a combination of all the above? Maybe, but what could explain his physical disappearance, the total absence of news? Nobody could tell.

Without thinking, she googled her own name, adding to it "Davos 2024". Tens of thousands of hits, algorithmically ranked with the help of generative AI, turned her feckless search into a doom loop. The first results were the craziest, all based on ludicrous conspiracy theories. She had neither the courage to scroll down nor the self-restraint to stop there. She ploughed on, googling "Helicopter crash Davos 2024". The results were as equally mind-numbing and senseless, conspiracy infused bunk. What was she doing? Why was she doing this at the risk of losing her mind? Muddying her own judgement and numbing her natural intuition.

Not only none the wiser, but rather at a complete loss, Olena turned to the traditional media, hoping to find there some incontrovertible evidence about what was going on. She put her trust in them to separate fiction from facts, fake news from the real thing. She clicked on a few websites. Davos was on the front page everywhere, left, right and centre. The events playing out in the Swiss mountain resort, whose very name was now synonymous with the global elite, were so extraordinary, so unthinkable, so beyond the realm of the expected, that nothing else seemed to matter. The world over, newspapers and TV channels would make a huge deal out of this for days to come. This was a story that would run and run, and yet, for the moment, the traditional media, despite their massive presence at the Circle and their unrivalled access to official and unofficial sources, could only know so much.

But amidst the excited hypothesising, two insights caught Olena's attention.

According to unnamed government sources quoted in several newspapers, shortly before flying to Davos, the helicopter pilot had spent time with a young woman in a bar. Efforts deployed to identify her had led to a dead-end. A few stories provided some juicy details. The pilot, emerging from a painful divorce and depicted as depressive by colleagues and friends, had met this lady on Tinder. Her identity was fake and the email IP address with which she'd created her Tinder account led to Poltavka, a village in Russia's far-east, right on the border with China. It seems they'd agreed to meet at a bar, where she'd spiked his non-alcoholic cocktail with a substance that would make him feel extremely unwell three hours later. She'd then evaporated into orchestrated-thin air. The effectiveness of both the substance and the young woman's disappearance were taken as proof that the helicopter accident could have only been the work of "an intelligence agency". Leading newspapers suggested a possible Russian lead. Not a surprise for Olena.

Another bunch of articles on the lockdown corroborated the first conclusions about a possible Russian involvement. Again, according to "credible government sources", Davos' total closure would be maintained until midday on Thursday despite the suspicion that the snipers and their support team had already left the valley. Swiss special mountain forces had followed their ski tracks near the Strela and Chüpfenflue peaks, which, on the other side of the mountain, plunged down the vertiginous slopes leading towards Schmitten, a calm, tiny village where locals had reported an unusual amount of car movement in the early morning. Most of the papers pointed out that, most likely, these individuals had prepared their escape days, if not weeks, in advance, had benefited from massive logistical support, and were by now in Liechtenstein or even Austria. Another reason to suspect a Russian lead, and to draw a cautious connection between the helicopter crash and the two shootings.

Olena closed her laptop. After almost three hours of reading, she knew a bit more but understood less. If the Russians had been after her, they'd have done a clean job. And what reason did they have to want her dead, apart from her nationality and her new job? OK, her fund stood to benefit from the recent decision to seize some Russian assets parked abroad, but surely this wasn't enough to want her eliminated. So, if she was a target, what could possibly be the motive? She was at a loss to identify anything that really held water. But what then was behind the series of dramatic events to which she had repeatedly found herself so physically close or embroiled in some way or another? A distant friend of hers and fellow Ukrainian had been amongst the victims of the helicopter crash, the young guy struck down yesterday by a mysterious disease had repeatedly asked her for a meeting. Mere coincidence felt like an inadequate explanation.

She opened the curtains. The nocturnal snow had given way to morning winter sunshine and an intense blue sky. A short distance away, the spectacularly beautiful Strela stood calm and majestic, its chiselled form clad in immaculate white. Strange to think that a commando of killers had passed at its foot a day earlier, she thought, before saying to herself: 'Time to go out, breathe some fresh air and get your head straight.'

*****

At 9am this morning, the habitually bustling Promenade was buzzing with activity of the most unusual kind.

Like every year, Davos' most prestigious street had been desecrated to make room for partner venues. For a week, old family businesses and traditional Graubünden eateries were quite literally taken over by the Circle's tech, financial and media partners. Akin to some kind of upmarket trade fair, all along the Promenade their global brands competed for visibility seeking to project power and influence. Unrestrained, unashamed, in the spirit of more is always more and bigger is always better! A straightforward transaction whereby the retailers, restaurants and bars at the epicentre of Davos' social life shifted to a different business model, earning a fortune in the process. Instead of selling their services, they did the opposite. They closed and rented out their space to the highest bidder, with the giants of the global economy outcompeting each other until settling on an egregious price. The rent economy *par excellence*. Earnings well in excess of what was economically or socially desirable, irking almost everyone– the locals (with the exception of the business owners on the Promenade of course), the partners, as well as all Circle participants. Too bad, but a cardinal rule of the Circle at play – money always has the last word.

That morning, the Promenade's shop fronts had been subject to further transformation. The recently installed prestigious brand names were now at best defaced, at worst completely concealed by flamboyant banners and painted placards. Olena stopped on Arkadenparkplatz. The logos of two famous tech brands currently riding high at the top of the SP500 had been upstaged by multiple posters daubed with hand painted red messages. "Climate Justice for All", said one. Others read "Reset the Circle", "One rule for the US, one rule for us!" and "Circle = American Pi" (that one was clever, she thought). As she walked down the Promenade absorbing the décor, Olena decided that while their wit and wisdom varied, all these impromptu outpourings voiced a common sentiment: enough is enough. An anti-Western stance and by association, anti-Circle too, appositely summed up by one of the funnier daubings:

"The Circle: Improving the State of YOUR World, not OURS. Signed: The REST".

Intrigued, Olena wondered how the fly-posters had got away with such an impressive display right under the noses of the cantonal police.

She only had to go a couple of hundred metres further down the Promenade for an answer. There, the same foreign minister who yesterday had taken to the plenary stage, was this morning in action on the streets of Davos, aided and abetted by fifty or so fellow participants. Just in front of Schneider's Restaurant, he was parleying with a police officer, his sacred white badge in full view and brandishing his diplomatic passport while others in the group were getting on with fixing their placards to the shop front.

Olena recognised several faces: the CEO of one of the largest Asian retailers, the dean of a prestigious Singaporean university, the finance ministers from two African countries who'd just defaulted on their debt, a central banker from Latin America, and a few more she couldn't put a name to, but whose faces she knew from the press. A good-humoured but resolute group of white badges, determined to be heard. The day before, like all other Circle mutineers, they'd been politely blocked by the police as soon as they'd started their freedom march in the direction of Klosters.

They'd retreated to the centre of town, deciding instead to take their campaign to the Promenade.

A little further down the street, Olena spotted another group of white badged participants fraternizing with climate justice demonstrators under the watchful eye of the police. As she passed by, they handed her a leaflet. She stopped and began to read: it was the copy of an op-ed published that morning in a prominent US newspaper. Its authors, three ministers present in Davos that day, argued that the Western bloc was no longer in a position of power, having lost both its absolute supremacy and the 'moral high ground' in the face of accusations of hypocrisy. They went on to accuse the Circle of being a mere mouthpiece for the Western bloc. Concluding with the damning line: "Throughout its history, the Circle has taken positive notions like 'inclusion', 'collaboration', 'partnership, 'equal justice', or 'equality' and turned them into empty words. It always says the right things, but what about acting on them?"

Olena looked around. Nobody seemed very interested. Passers-by on their way to the Congress Centre walked with their heads down and shoulders bowed, against both the biting cold and any unwanted attention. They looked either preoccupied or studiedly indifferent. The previous days' events had left their mark.

Law enforcement agencies were on edge. So was everybody else.

*****

Olena continued on her way. As she was crossing Kurgatenstrasse, a man suddenly appeared at her side. Tall with dark glasses masking a large part of his face, wearing a bulky, quilted jacket, half-open.

'Miss Kostarenko: Phillip Tiddlethwait would like a word. Would you mind following me?'

Olena had seen enough movies to understand the meaning of a half-open jacket in freezing temperatures. She took a furtive look around, before asking, unable to disguise the panic in her voice:

'Where to?'

'Just over there', responded the man, gesturing with his head to a car parked on the pavement a few metres away.

She looked at it. Black, luxurious, massive. Anywhere else it might have been conspicuous, but not in Davos in the third week of January. Her first instinctive reaction was to read the number plate: "GE-01-72". This didn't go unnoticed.

'The vehicle of His Majesty's Ambassador to the UN in Geneva', said the man, before adding with a polite but firm voice: 'Please hurry up Miss Kostarenko, diplomatic plates or not, we can't stay on the pavement indefinitely.'

Several men and two women were standing in the street not far from the car, watching her. Olena suddenly worried that the whole thing was a set-up. But if it was, what could she do?

'How can I be sure Phillip, Mr. Tiddlethwait, is in there? Why doesn't he come to me?'

'Quickly Miss Kostarenko. We don't have much time.'

She followed him, trembling, not knowing what she was doing or why. Her 'escort' opened the left rear door of the waiting car.

She got in as if on autopilot. Phillip was sitting in the front passenger seat, on the right. Behind him, and now next to her, was a man holding a submachine. He hadn't reacted as she'd sat down, his unswerving gaze fixed upon what was going on outside the car. The driver set off immediately. Phil turned to greet her.

'Hi Olia'.

'Phillip (diminutives seemed inappropriate at that moment), what the f---k is going on?

The car turned left on to Tallstrasse, four huge black SUVs forming a convoy around them, two in front and two behind. The one just ahead bore diplomatic plates with the number 9. They headed in the direction of the lake.

'Who are they? Who are you come to that?'

'American colleagues. Looking after us.'

He paused for a second. The convoy was driving fast down the empty streets.

'Olia: I work for the good guys. You must trust me on that. It's all I can tell you for the moment. The less you know the safer you are. You can see we have had a bit of a situation here. I won't claim to have the full picture now, but we may be talking about acts of war.'

'War?'

'Yes. At war. Here in Davos. A war different from yours, back in Ukraine. But a war nonetheless.'

'What do you mean? You're not making any sense Phil. I don't understand. What the hell has this got to do with me?'

'There are so many people involved that sooner than we think, the full details of what has been going on will be exposed. My cover will be blown. For the moment, better to remain discreet.'

They'd reach a field next to Davosersee, surrounded by a double row of barbed wire. A soldier in military fatigue opened the gate. They entered and parked.

'Where are we? What are we doing here?'

'We're on the site of a state-of-the-art anti-aircraft installation manned by the Swiss army. It's set up for the duration of the meeting, to protect the town against a possible suicide attack from the air, or a missile. Consider it as my certificate of authenticity for you – if I wasn't who I say I am, they would never have let me in. We are safe here.'

They both got out of the car and Phillip walked round to face Olena. She saw in his eyes an air of seriousness and steely determination she'd never discerned before. He took her hands.

'You're freezing', he said.

'I'm petrified with fear', she confessed but managing a smile.

'Olia: we are going to need your help.'

'You must be joking! My help with what? What could I possibly do?'

'To complete the jigsaw. To unearth the missing pieces.'

She glanced at him with fear and curiosity in equal measure.

'That sounds way above my pay grade, I'm not sure I'm capable.'

'Of course, you are. Let me explain. The helicopter, the shootings – we understand what's going on and are taking the appropriate measures to deal with the situation. But there are two things that bother us because they don't fit the picture.'

'What?'

'The death of Alain Girard and the attempt to poison Mark Massover… He died late yesterday, not from poisoning, but brain damage.'

'I didn't know that', she murmured with a shiver.

'Both are connected to you Olia. In both cases, we are talking about the same 'signature', an organophosphate'.

She gazed into his eyes.

'Do you know why 'me'?'

'I don't. And that's why I need your help.'

'What is it you need me to do?'

'Continue to turn up at the Congress Centre and do all within your power to keep the project with Karl Manhof alive.'

She let out a nervous little laugh.

'Are you crazy? How can I do that with everything that's happened? Am I just going to call him and say: "Hey Karl, I know things have gone a bit pear shaped and deathly quiet on the professional front, but we're both still here in Davos, so are a bunch of others and Zelenskyy is on his way. How about you and I make like nothing much has happened and resume pitching?"'

'Exactly!' said Philip ignoring the sarcasm. 'If anyone can pull it off, you can. You know you can. Please try. You risk nothing. And if you feel vulnerable, you'll have discreet guardian angels everywhere', he gestured towards the dozen or so figures gathered around the SUVs.

He kissed her on the cheek, before handing her a brooch of cabochon turquoise stones set in yellow gold, the colours of Ukraine.

'Pretty, isn't it? Show it off tomorrow pinned to your chest, please. You'll be our eyes and ears, and we'll never be far away.'

Day 7

Friday 19 January 2024

Davos

Under normal circumstances, the last day of the annual meeting was a *piano*, almost dull, affair; sometimes redeemed by a carefully composed *crescendo* moment to finish. This year, the circumstances were so extraordinary that it was anything but *piano,* and as for the carefully composed *crescendo,* it looked doomed to become either a deafening silence or an all-too audible cacophony.

The dramas of the past week had thrown the Circle into a state of unprecedented disarray. The august institution had met its iceberg and was listing ineluctably. And yet, the Don stood firm on the bridge of his sinking ship, engaged up to the very last in a desperate attempt to salvage what he could. In a dogged bid to make it look as if he was still in command of something, the Don had ordered the Circle's programme team to pull together overnight a new set of sessions for the final day, making use of anyone who might still be around. The result: a random and ragged line-up ranging from fintech and fine art to conscious capitalism and the US election. A last-ditch attempt to give the day a semblance of normalcy. But, as for the concluding plenary, the likelihood of President Zelenskyy being there seemed to be diminishing with every passing minute.

Yesterday, at midday sharp, the lockdown lifted, and an exodus had begun, with numerous participants taking to their heels, deserting Davos in a bumper-to-bumper convoy of black limousines. Most of them doubtful they'd be rushing back to the Magic Mountain any time soon. But there were those who chose not to vacate the valley. They included senior executives of companies that had committed significant parts of their marketing budgets to what were now graffiti-strafed shopfronts on a deserted street. Reluctant to cut their losses quite yet, they were still hoping for a miracle in the form of a return on their investment. Hard cash would be best, but even some reputational kudos, by mere virtue of having been there at such a 'historical' juncture, would be better than nothing. Others stayed because they had business to conclude. Some lingered on simply out of morbid curiosity, like onlookers at the scene of a particularly gruesome pile-up, unsettled yet excited by the impression that they were part of something bigger than themselves.

There was definite attrition in the quantity and quality of those still in Davos by the time Friday morning came. But there were more than enough to make things look viable. This assorted bunch, now calling themselves 'remainers', gravitated to the Congress Centre as soon as it opened. For once, it was the place to be, but surreal, not *realpolitik*, came closer to describing the prevailing atmosphere. The public areas, normally the networking nexus, were all but empty, except for a few white badge first timers. This group of hapless individuals, neither movers nor shakers, who'd ended up at the Circle almost by accident, were continuing they own personal charade of doing anything they could to convey an impression of busyness in the now deserted 'corridors of power'.

In the café corners, it was a different story altogether – the conversation here was buzzier and busier than on a usual meeting day. Rumours ran rife. Caffeine-fuelled, the fierce senior execs and powerbrokers were discussing with excessive excitement the 'latest' about what had been going on. The perennial bunch of alpha-male know-it-all monopolized the floor, every one of them in possession of a dark secret they were only too willing to share, always long on hints of some sort of plot, but always short on any evidence to back it up. Anybody party to these bombastic exchanges found themselves over- yet ill-informed and in a state of enhanced confusion as to who lay behind the events of the past week. The hypotheses on offer included: America's CIA and FBI, Russia's FSB, SVR, and GRU, the Mossad, China's MSS, the French secret service, or the Brits'. It could also have been the nefarious work of the far-right, or the far-left. Or maybe that of the secret globalist cabal against which the MAGA crowd and the QAnons of this world had raged ever since the publication of a certain book by the Don? In this melee of rumours and confusion, everybody had a theory and an explanation. Truth be told, nobody knew. Everybody was at a loss. Only one thing remained certain - as always there was an army of spies in action at Davos.

*****

Olena saw Karl from a distance, at the entrance of the Seehorn room. He was on his phone, and something in his body language made her feel he was not his usual self. As out of character as it might be, Olena thought Karl looked nervous. The veneer of pride and self-confidence had slipped. He saw her and hung up. She joined him.

'Hi Karl, how are you doing?'

She didn't wait for an answer and continued:

'I'm quite tempted by the session on Trump. Do you wanna come with me? It's happening just in there and is only due to last 45 minutes. What do you think – might be interesting?'

'OK – why not', he said distractedly before taking a grip and adding with almost excess attention: 'That's very pretty – and very patriotic', gesturing to the turquoise and gold brooch (echoing the colours of the Ukrainian flag) that was now pinned to Olena's black cashmere rollneck. 'I didn't have you down as jewellery sort-of-girl!'

'It's not every day that I prepare to meet my president, though it does happen quite often, I admit. Still, no harm in a subtle show of solidarity on foreign soil.'

'Gotcha.'

They sat next to each other at the back of the room. The session had just started and the exchange between two Americans, an academic and a hedge fund manager, was already heating up. The scholar was arguing that any pretence that the November election would be an election like any other, was madness - it would not be.

He went on to elaborate: 'The outcome of this election is not even in the hands of the 160 million strong American electorate. No! It stands to be decided by just tens of thousands of voters in a handful of swing states. And yet the result will affect eight billion people worldwide. Why? Because we, the American people, are about to elect a fascist', he warned, eyeballing his audience, 'who, from day one, will subvert American democracy by abusing the power of the office of the president. Name me any other presidential frontrunner who's been impeached twice and promised to target political opponents and to seek retribution if elected?' he asked rhetorically with a defiant look in his eyes.

'This is ludicrous,' retorted the investor. 'Take a step back. When he was President, Trump was kind of right about many things. And if he wins the election, it will be an example of democracy in action. The American institutions are strong enough to prevent a slide into autocracy.'

The room laughed. So did Olena.

There was more to come. The moderator, a seasoned political journalist, turned to the investor and asked him whether he was aware of a statement that Dan Murphy, the US banker gunned down three days earlier, had made shortly before coming to Davos. At a professional conference in New York, he'd been asked what a Trump victory would mean for the US economy and the financial markets. 'His response was this', the moderator said putting on his glasses and consulting his notes : “A Trump presidency would be destructive and ultimately disastrous, not only for the US but also for the rest of the world, because it would undermine the rule of law, the *sine qua non* of our capitalist system. Trump poses a fundamental threat to the future of our country as we know it. Once in the White House, the methods he is likely to deploy would negatively impact all the basic decisions that underpin a functioning economy: hiring, investing, valuing assets, consumer behaviour and much more beyond. It would be a catastrophe. Therefore, we must do everything we can to prevent a Trump victory.” The moderator closed his notebook, looked out at the room, and then turning to the investor asked:

‘Do you agree?’

‘No, I don’t. And let me tell you, many top investors and bankers in my country don’t either. Dan’s opinion, God rest his soul, was nothing if not a bit extreme.’

At that moment, a political-plot-shaped penny dropped for many in the room, including Olena. A young woman from the audience stood up and addressing the panel, said out loud what all of them were thinking.

‘After what we just heard, can the twin shootings here in Davos, of a democratic Congressman and this banker who professed such an anti-Trump position, be a coincidence? Could there be a partisan political subtext? What do the panellists think?’

'Now that's a question. This really is the most interesting Circle in years!' observed the moderator with a wry smile. 'Who'd like to take this question?'

Before anyone could respond, eight men - five in civilian clothes and three wearing the uniform of the Graubünden cantonal police - stormed into the room. Seven of them rushed straight towards two participants seated at the outer end of the front row, grabbing them by the shoulders before handcuffing and hooding them with no questions asked. The eighth stepped on to the stage, seized the mike from the moderator, and announced in perfect English with an air of absolute authority and no irony:

'Ladies and gentlemen: We apologise for the interruption. Just a routine police operation that will only take a moment. I wish you an excellent session.'

Restoring the microphone to the momentarily speechless moderator, he joined his colleagues, and they left the room with the same efficiency as they'd entered it, taking with them the two handcuffed individuals, whose faces, now hooded, were hidden from view.

*****

The moderator cut the session short. After a moment of shocked suspended animation, the Seehorn descended in bedlam. Most were now on their feet and almost all using unacceptably loud voices, either asking frantically who the two arrested were or asserting equally noisily that they knew exactly who they were.

Some people in the room had seen their badges or met them. It took just a few minutes to confirm their identity, and only a few more minutes for the whole world, courtesy of social media, to know who they were. Both had the same profile – oligarchs and billionaires; one from Ukraine and the other from Slovakia. Rich and famous in their own way. They'd benefited from the sell-off of state assets after the dissolution of USSR and made a fortune. Twenty years or so later, they'd converted money into power. The Circle was a necessary stepping stone towards respectability.

'What did you make of that?', Karl asked Olena as they made their way out of the room.

'The police, you mean? Certainly not a routine happening in my experience.'

'This Ukrainian oligarch… Is he a friend of yours?'

'A friend, no, but I know him by sight and I know he's got clout. In 2021, when Ukraine passed a "de-oligarchisation" law forcing all oligarchs to disclose their assets and stop funding political parties, I thought he'd be arrested, but somehow, he slipped through the net.'

'How come? Western countries won't fund your reconstruction and let you into the EU if they believe that oligarchs like him pocket the proceeds.'

'Of course, we know that all too well! But confronting the oligarchs is a risky business. Ask our former central banker. She did. Then had to flee to London where a mystery car collision put her in a wheelchair. A few weeks later, a Molotov cocktail burnt down her house outside Kyiv. A very risky business Karl.'

She paused for a second, before adding: 'Anyway, his arrest here in Davos has nothing to do with all that, but I'm sure the real reason will come to light soon.'

They'd now left the Seehorn room, but the frenzy followed them. This year the surprises just kept coming and the atmosphere at the Circle was reaching fever point. Olena needed some space – mental and physical. She pulled Karl aside, looking for a quieter spot where she could hear herself think and they could be more easily seen. She then asked him point-blank:

'What happened with Mark Massover, the head of Carbon Markets Integrity? I thought you might have an idea'.

He stiffened. Almost but not quite imperceptibly, but Olena hadn't missed it.

'What am I supposed to know? I don't even know him.'

'That he was poisoned two days ago and died as a result of concussion yesterday. I am surprised you hadn't seen anything – it was on the news'.

'Missed it, then,' Karl said sulkily.

'Really? Don't you talk to anyone either?'

'Olenka: I'm in Davos to work, with you and with others. I am here to do business. I don't have time for gossip.'

'Well… It's gossip that cost the life of someone who'd been trying to talk to me ever since I got here.'

'Why are you telling me all this?' he asked with a trace of unease in his voice.

'I'm not sure Karl… Just want to sound you out. You know what they say: a worry shared is a worry halved.'

Olena was silent for a few seconds, concentration intensifying the green of her eyes, and spoke again.

'Despite the mayhem, you and I have had some useful meetings. Even so, what the immediate future for the project will look like is anyone's guess. But, whatever, I wanted to go back to our conversation on the train last Saturday. You suggested then that your full support depended on my acceptance of your offsetting certification business.'

'I wasn't that categoric, I didn't say dealbreaker. But it would be a nice … let's say, bonus."

He stopped for a second, wondering if he could be overheard by the couple standing down the hallway, decided not, and carried on.

'I understand your worry about bogus credits, blowback, conflicts of interest, fraud, all of that. You are right. I agree that existing carbon credit markets are often grossly manipulated and don't get me started on net-zero claims. Welcome to the green world! But this is different. I'm different Olenka. Your country is so rich in resources around agriculture, forestry, and renewable energy that I could generate carbon credits easily and on a broad scale. And I'd do this properly of course. I mean… cleanly, no corruption. You know as well as me that my reputation is all I have.'

'So, you want to make money twice, with your Ukraine fund, and with your offsetting certification business, one selling to the other. Won't you be facing a mammoth conflict of interest?'

'Not really…' The voice was hesitant. 'It depends how you look at it. And there'll be a Chinese wall between the two.'

Olena smiled.

'I can look at it any way I like, and I'll always see a conflict of interest. By the way, we never got a chance to discuss the governance of this new Ukrainian fund you'll put together. What's that going to look like?'

'Ah! That should re-assure you and lay to rest all those concerns you expressed in Dubai and that I sense you still have. My idea is to set up a foundation.'

She cut him off. 'A not-for-profit you mean?'

'Exactly right. A not-for-profit that will oversee the fund for when the capital invested in Ukraine starts generating a return, which is going to take a while as we know. A board will oversee the foundation to make sure that the Ukrainian fund is used only for the benefit of Ukraine. Accountable for future bottom-line profit if you wish. And cherry on the cake, it could also be the guarantor of best practices with the offsetting certification business,' before adding in a sarcastic tone: 'with your permission – if it ever sees the light of the day.'

'And who'll be on the board of this foundation?'

'I have several names in mind. As the main provider of capital, I'll be its chairman. I've approached a few people who expressed an interest. Some have already confirmed. A famous academic from my own country, Germany, whose name I cannot reveal yet, but very big! And a former colleague of yours. He now sits on the Circle's managing board. Perfect candidate, plus a few others. The board must be lean, five or six in total. You could be one of them, Olenka,' he concluded, his arrogant and oh-so-pleased-with-himself veneer back in place.

'I see…Thank you,' she nodded, baffled by the crudeness of his proposal. 'I need to go to the bathroom and then get a bit of fresh air. I'll see you in a bit.'

As she walked up from the bowels of the Congress Centre to the Promenade, everything suddenly became clear. Karl's few words about the foundation board had served as an eye-opener. His proposal defied the laws of corporate physics: a brilliant academic who knew nothing about business, an ex-colleague famed for his mediocrity and pliability, the ill-disguised attempt to bribe her… Karl, the little bully with a big wallet, thought he could do anything he wanted.

Pushing open the heavy door on to the street, she was met by an icy blast of cold air. That morning, Davos was in the grips of a whirling snowstorm. She pulled her fur hat down and her jacket collar up against the blizzard and strode on.

The biting chill of the wind and snow outside were competing with incandescent anger boiling up from within. Pure, unadulterated anger – directed at Karl for sure, but mostly at herself. What a fool she'd been.

Death, doubt, deceit, duplicity, disappointment, (wheeler)-dealing, danger – D for Davos. It'd been a harrowing experience, but the week was coming to an end and things were surely coming to a head.

Epilogue

Wednesday 24 January 2024
Geneva

The Don's face filled the whole screen before the image zoomed out to show him seated at an imposing desk with his hands clasped. A little ill at ease, and despite the years of accumulated experience, still characteristically gauche. Through the large smoked glass French window behind him, it was possible to discern the Jura mountains in the distance and Lake Geneva glinting in the foreground.

The anodyne music that had accompanied the opening image faded and was replaced by a voice-over question. Those in the know would recognize Sandra's American accent tempered with deference. She asked:

'Sir: what are your thoughts and feelings in response to the events surrounding your chief of staff – Phillip Tiddlethwait?'

'A terrible, shocking disappointment. Betrayal! Tiddlethwait had worked as my righthand man for two years, recommended to me by a senior British banker who's been a regular at Davos for decades. I thought of him as a friend of the Circle, and I made the big mistake of trusting this man. This, by the way, is illustrative of the porous membrane that exists between big business and the intelligence services in the United Kingdom.'

'Why sir, and why do you call it a mistake?'

'Because Tiddlethwait wasn't working in my office, he was working as a spy, in my office,' the emotion in his voice revealed how much the Don regarded what had happened as a personal affront to himself - a matter of betrayal and profound disloyalty. The Don went on to elaborate. 'He was "planted" to plunder my data. Both from my phone and from personal meetings. You see, they've found recording devices in my private office. Over the last 24 months, the person holding the most sensitive position at the Circle, the one that requires utmost trust and confidence, was in fact a traitor in our midst.'

The disembodied interviewer went on:

'What was the objective of this data theft from your personal contacts?'

'To gain access to the phones of a highly sensitive and influential community of individuals, to install a "zero-click" spyware that then, undetectable, goes on to hack all future activity on the mobile phones targeted.'

'Like Pegasus, the Israeli software?' asked the voice-over. 'To covertly record emails, phone calls and text messages?'

'I presume so', responded the Don with contrition in his voice. 'I assume this dreadful surveillance technology has been used to spy on all my contacts. I profoundly apologize to every one of them, and I will hold MI6 and the

British government to account', he declared solemnly, his gaze fixed on the invisible camera.

Suddenly the soundtrack music resumed and for a minute or so, a series of informal images of celebrities, all instantly recognisable global movers and shakers, taken at recent Circle gatherings, scrolled across the screen. As suddenly as it had disappeared, the distinctive, balding egg-shaped oval face of the Don reclaimed the screen, and the sycophantic questioning resumed:

'Sir, must we assume that all these people are now being spied on by MI6 at the bidding of their US pay masters. He who pays the piper…?'

The Don took a deep breath, before answering with resignation:

'What can I say? But highly likely: yes.'

'I see…,' said a formless 'Sandra' with a perceptible, albeit invisible, knowing nod. 'And now sir, may we turn to the subject that has preoccupied the media – social and otherwise for the past week. The unanswered questions of why your chief of staff disappeared in Davos a few days ago and to where did he disappear? Sir, do you have any answers?'

'I do and I don't. It will be for the Swiss authorities to elaborate in greater detail as and when. But for the moment, I can only say that he was involved in activities that I find deeply shocking and therefore denounce in the strongest possible terms.'

'Can you be more specific sir?'

'Phillip Tiddlethwait was…' he hesitated for one second before correcting himself: '… is, an active, professional agent, not a simple informant. He was trained to engage in a mission highly detrimental to the interests of the Circle. Apart from what I described as his activities while in my executive office at the Circle – spying on me and my network –, some media sources are saying that he was tasked during this year's annual meeting in Davos to retrieve compromising material concerning the former US president…'

'Donald Trump, you mean'.

'Yes, President Trump. But it might well be that no such material exists at all. I mean, it could be just fiction… It could be that Mr. Tiddlethwait was engaged in some quite other nefarious activity, the origins of which I know nothing about..., settling old scores or something of that nature. A "covert operation", as they say. But I simply don't know and can only repeat with caution the gist of the story gleaned in private conversations with people whose profession it is to know this sort of thing.'

He paused, perhaps for effect, before adding somewhat mechanically:

'Among the Swiss authorities, in particular. In any case, something clearly went wrong for Mr. Tiddlethwait. He's disappeared and nobody knows where he is, and I'm not sure we'll ever know.'

'Do you think he's still alive?'

'For his sake, I hope so', the Don responded with the shadow of an ambivalent smile.

'And what about the two Americans shot in Davos, the Democrat from Congress and Dan Murphy, the senior banker? And before that, the helicopter crash?'

'I don't think we've heard the last word on this. I can only share with you what I was told. This is not that simple. Not simple at all', he stressed. 'There are still many grey areas, such as the bullets fired for example, they were of a sort exclusively used by NATO forces. I find this information surprising and perturbing. Doesn't such a double bluff make it too obvious? Russia was immediately singled out, but as I just said, there is surely much more to the story. As for the helicopter crash, I am told this was just a tragic coincidence. A very unfortunate accident caused by the psychological condition of the pilot. He had personal issues and had started to drink, you see… Finding the truth is never simple. I think we are in a "wilderness of mirrors" that captures the imagination of spy-novel enthusiasts.'

*****

Olena discarded the iPad, taking care it didn't fall off the bed. Exhaling in disbelief, she fell back on to the pile of crumpled feather pillows and stretched. She was naked. So too was Phillip who was lying beside her, watching her watching the video. He then got up and pulled on his boxers before drawing the curtains. The lake shimmered in the morning light, mirror-like. From the vantage point of their safe house, an elegant apartment on the fifth floor on Quai Gustave Ador, all seemed peaceful. Indeed, notwithstanding the harrowing week that had preceded the night they had just enjoyed together, a sentiment of unassailable tranquillity could have infused that bright winter morning on the banks of Lake Geneva. Phillip came back to bed, laying his head on Olena's shoulder. She turned to him.

'Bloody hell! What is this all about? I don't have the courage to watch the last ten minutes.'

'A quasi perfect deepfake. The proof that AI evolves at a breath-taking speed. This video is amazing in its disturbing perfection. For those of us who know the Don well, there are still a few unnatural, or odd, facial expressions and unusual eye movements, but the rest is beyond reproach, including the lip pinching, and the absence of distortions around his face. The background defies reality – it's just like being in his office. It's a work of art. Russian, undoubtedly.'

'But surely deepfake detection tools will call it out …'

'Who cares? Too late. I'm the one who's been outed. The damage is done. This deepfake is so effective, a blueprint in *disinformatsiya*: a potent mix of insinuations, half-truths, outright lies, admissions and denials. Watching it, you don't know what to believe and what not to believe. It subtly sows the seeds of doubt and creates confusion.'

'Maybe, but not everybody will fall for it, surely.'

'Of course not. Not everybody. But it doesn't need to be everybody. A few is enough. The difference is always made at the margins. The million or so likes from the 60 million who've already viewed it on YouTube and X is more than ample. And it was only posted yesterday!'

Olena propped herself up against the pillows, before observing:

'There's a certain irony that according to the Circle's Risks analysis released last week at Davos, misinformation and disinformation will be the number one risk over the next two years.'

'Yes. The Don was prescient, but not protected. And this is only the beginning. Already there are two other deepfake videos starring the Don; same format, same effect. One about colonialism and the global south and another about the plutocrats who come to the Circle. They are so well done and so damming as to beg the question: can the Don and his precious Circle recover from this? In a few short months, AI-generated media will become undetectable, videos like these will pass unhindered into the realm of 'truth'. You can be certain that we'll be inundated by this fake stuff courtesy of the Russian regime and anybody else with a vested interest in bringing our democratic world to its knees.'

She reached for his hand and kissed it. Then got up to get dressed in front of him, naturally, as she had in the past.

'What are you going to do Phil?'

'Ask me in a few days! My cover has been blown. And the whole truth will emerge, inevitably.'

She shot a troubled questioning glance at him, her green eyes looking straight into his.

'What is the truth?'

'Here's my version of the truth. There'll be so many variations on the theme over the coming days, let me get mine in first.'

He got up in his turn, kissed her on the forehead.

'While in Davos, I was supposed to get a document so compromising for Trump as to make him unelectable'.

'What is it?'

'This I can't tell, but you know that Trump travelled to Moscow on several occasions before becoming president. The Russians are smart. They are experts at accumulating *kompromat* just in case. This goes for anybody who might become interesting later. It's a long game. All that's needed is patience, and occasionally it yields benefits well worth the wait. They are good at that.'

'Phil! Don't forget I am Ukrainian with two Russian grandparents. I understand this sort of stuff.'

'Of course you do! Stupid of me Olia.'

He went to the window, glanced at the street. It was a warm winter morning. There were joggers running along the lake, children bicycling, groups of tourists admiring Geneva's famous water jet, lovers strolling arm-in-arm.

Five floors below their safe house, people were getting on with their lives with disarming normalcy. Uncomplicated destinies. He turned to Olia silhouetted against the milky morning sunlight.

'You heard and read about the "Anything but Trump" initiative?'

'Of course, I did. It's everywhere.'

'I'm part of it. More than a part in fact; I'm an essential cog in its whole machinery. Long story short: at the very moment that I was about to get hold of this notorious piece of information, the "proof" as we called it, I was 'welcomed' by a group of *spetsnaz* who had no intention of sharing anything with me, except a well-aimed bullet. In all likelihood, our agent in Moscow, who was supposed to procure this vital file and get it to us, had been turned. Anyway, I escaped and here I am!'

'And what about the two Americans? And the helicopter crash?'

'We were a major group of the "Anything but Trump" initiative devotees in Davos, and the opposition had fielded an equally significant team whose sole purpose was to keep an eye on us, and in the end take action. For example, the two oligarchs arrested during your Trump session on Friday, they were part of this group. Small cogs; informants to the Kremlin. Planted at the Circle to listen and report. And maybe more than that. Who knows? We haven't figured it out yet.'

'Oh right', observed Olena with an indifferent tone, as if this wasn't a real surprise.

'Putin is a gambler. When I told you in Davos that we are at war, I meant it, literally. Putin has just launched a new front in his crusade against the west, right under our very noses. We didn't see it coming and we don't yet fully understand where it will lead. We keep misreading his intentions.'

Olena nodded, before observing:

'You are right Phil. If what you describe is correct, it will be like Ukraine two years ago. Until the minute the war started, nearly everyone, including myself, had misread Putin's intentions. We believed he would never launch a full-scale invasion, assuming instead he'd opt for what he's good at: proxy warfare, cyber-attacks, and all the other covert ploys he's been practising his entire career at the KGB.'

Phillip stood silent, leaning against the wall, with a dark reflective look in his eyes, and spoke again:

'Exactly! And not only is Putin a gambler, but he's grown into an ever-higher-stakes gambler. He is a reckless gambler! Doing things that look senseless to us is his metier, he can't help it. What he's done at Davos - organising a helicopter crash, the shooting of two prominent US citizens, and the attempt to get rid of me - is proof of that. It sounds unbelievable that he could be so bold, that he could take such a huge risk; but he must have judged that the whole mess confronting the Biden administration at this very moment – Israel, Iran's provocations, the Houthis in the Red Sea, your war Olia, and the difficulties in securing funding for your country, the Taiwanese elections, plus the other elements in this interminable list of issues, were diverting US attention, and therefore offering an opportunity for mammoth risk-taking. He is reckless, but not stupid. What happened in Davos last week is just the beginning. He's playing on our fears of a wider war, and he must have thought it was the right time to try his luck. The downing of the helicopter and the shootings are a warning. Terrifying! Imagine that he did not hesitate to kill five aboard the helicopter to get just one target: the young English socialite. She was one of "ours"; the four others were innocent collateral damage if I may put it that way. So, between her and the shootings, he picked on three critical nodes in our "Anything but Trump" network, knowing exactly what he was doing. The young British woman, the congressman and the senior banker were aware of this famous compromising document and were ready to use it: the congressman among policymakers, the CEO among business leaders and the young Brit among influencers in the US and Europe. With their murders, Putin is sending us a stark message: "Nothing will stop me. Let me show you what I'm capable of. Don't mess with me. I'm playing the long game and gambling on a Trump return in November. And as you now know, I'm ready to go to great lengths to support my friend Donald.'"

It was all too familiar to Olena who felt the need to resort to humour. Smiling, she asked:

'Have you heard the one about what the MAGA crowd are calling Trump?'

'Not sure I have…'

'0047, because if he wins, he'll become America's 47th President and will ride to the rescue of the US, as 007 did for England. Well… We in Ukraine think he'll rescue Putin too."

*****

They sat on the sofa, their legs intertwined and holding hands, each lost in their own thoughts. Olena broke the silence first.

'I still have difficulties coming to terms with what you told me yesterday', she said in a whisper.

'About what?'

'Karl Manhof.'

'Are you that surprised? A cynical, cold-blooded, 'fad-dist'… A shit by any other name!'

'Sure! But not enough to want to murder me!'

'I told you what I thought Olia. He didn't want to murder you. He just wanted to incapacitate you and scare Mark Massover. You because you were an obstacle to his offset certification plan, and Massover because he had evidence of Karl's corruption. That's it. The whole plan was conducted with unbelievable incompetence, relying on this mediocre network of half-corrupt half-official former

KGB agents who keep poisoning people all over the place with mixed results. Anyway, I'll spare you the details, but you can stop worrying. Karl has been arrested and after his trial stands to spend a good spell behind bars. It's over. Karl Manhof was an almost irrelevant – not for you of course! - appendix to this whole saga.'

Olena stared at Phillip, trying to reassure herself he was telling the truth, the whole truth, and that she really had nothing more to fear. Then she looked away and asked:

'Call me crazy, but you know what I'd love to do?'

'Tell me.'

'Go for a walk in the woods behind the Circle's building, where you and I used to go at lunchtime. I loved it so much then and I need it now. Just you, me and the trees. Can we do that?'

'Course we can. But our guardian angels will have to come too. They can hide behind the trees!'

She managed a melancholic smile.

They left the building through a small service exit on to the rue Merle-d'Aubigné. Two huge black SUVs were waiting for them. They got into the first one. The car turned left, passed the sumptuous parc de la Grange and immediately headed up the hill.

'We are going to drive straight passed our old office – it seems that we've come full circle. That's weird.'

They never got there. Drawing near to the Circle head-quarters, a police car flagged them down. The road was being cordoned off, with dozens of police vehicles approaching, their sirens blaring. A helicopter was circling overhead. Clearly, a massive police operation was underway.

'What the f…k is going on?' asked Olena, turning to Phillip.

'Your guess is as good as mine.'

She wanted to believe him, but didn't. She took his hand and said with emotion but without conviction:

'Please say this is the last, concluding, episode.'

'Perhaps', murmured Phillip, squeezing Olena's hand.

If only she knew, he thought, and chose to put it down to a failure of imagination.